ESCAPE CLAUSES

Bob Payne
ESCAPE CLAUSES

Getting Away With a Travel Writing Life

— A 142-COUNTRY MEMOIR —

Bob Carries On Media, LLC

Copyright © 2022 Bob Payne
ALL RIGHTS RESERVED

Softcover
ISBN 978-0-578-86961-2

Ebook
ISBN 979-8-218-07439-5
ASIN B09TBZZ328

Published in the United States
by Bob Carries On Media, LLC
Scottsdale, Arizona
www.bobcarrieson.com

No part of this book may be reproduced, or stored in a retrieval system, or transmitted in any form or by any means, electronic, mechanical, photocopying, recording, or otherwise, without express written permission of the publisher.

Cover image by David Astley (banyanman) from Pixabay

ACKNOWLEDGEMENTS

I'm delighted and grateful that portions of this work were originally published in: *Aqua* (chapter 20); *BobCarriesOn.com* (chapter 26); *Bon Appétit* (chapter 10); *Condé Nast Traveler*, (chapters 3, 6, 14-16, 18, 20-21, 23-25); *iExplore.com* (chapter 4); *Islands* (chapters 7, 9, 11-13, 19-22); *Sail* (chapters 3, 17); *The Boston Globe* (chapters 4 5); *The International Railway Traveler* (chapter 5); *The Ritz-Carlton Magazine* (chapter 26); *The Tampa Times* (chapter 2); *The Walking Magazine* (chapter 5); and *Travel-Holiday* (chapter 4).

DEDICATION

For my Great Uncle Wilson,
who was a little different,
and sometimes more than a little.

TABLE OF CONTENTS

1 | *Stories That Came Before* — 11

2 | *Distant Music Only Some Can Hear* — 19

3 | *Introducing the Maldives* — 24

4 | *Stoned in Egypt, But Not in a Good Way* — 34

5 | *The Not So Rapido to Puerto Montt* — 42

6 | *Waving Goodbye From Robinson Crusoe's Island* — 47

7 | *The Lost Razor Blades of Zanzibar* — 57

8 | *Life, Death, and Rejection on the Amazon* — 69

9 | *Bora Bora Might Just Be Home* — 84

10 | *Food Writer? Martinique? You Bet!* — 96

11 | *Headhunters Laughed at What I Paid for My Wife* — 103

12 | *In the Seychelles, Every Position Is Paintable* — 114

13 | *Listening to the Greeks* — 128

14 | *To the North Pole Without Eating the Dogs* — 141

15 | *The Bikini Test* — 155

16	*In Antarctica, Take Only Photos, and Fuel Hose*	168
17	*Him? He's Just the Dad*	178
18	*My Expense Account Tattoo*	184
19	*Turtles for Ancestors*	189
20	*Favorite Near-death Experiences*	200
21	*When Do You Know You've Been There?*	208
22	*Easter Island: a Mystery Solved, a World Found*	216
23	*Bali After the Bombing*	221
24	*My Limp? Dogsled Accident. In Greenland*	229
25	*Camp Jaguar. All Welcome. Except for Snakes*	242
26	*The Places Farther Out*	254
	About The Author	259
	Praise for the Author	261

ESCAPE CLAUSES

1
Stories That Came Before

When people ask how you get started as a travel writer, I often tell them that running away from home at fifteen and hitchhiking alone around America is what worked for me.

I was gone for a summer on that first solo journey, thumbing my way from Miami, Florida, to Yellowstone National Park and then across the northern border states to Maine before heading south and home again. Along the way I would often help drivers stay awake and sometimes earn myself a meal by giving them someone to tell their stories to.

"I once had a dog," a story might begin. And soon enough, another fifty or a hundred miles of highway would be behind us, and I'd have one more story to tell as part of my own.

For more than half a century, listening to strangers in far places and making their stories a part of my own has allowed me to live a travel writing life.

It is a life in which I have visited 140-something countries, won a few travel writing awards, and seen my name appear in some good publications. Including *Condé Nast Traveler* magazine, where I spent a decade as a contributing editor and where I remain, I believe, the only writer of theirs ever to put the cost of a Polynesian tattoo on an expense report.

But time is telling me that if I want to share, once again, some of the stories that have become part of my own, I need to get busy. Even if those stories are now often about journeys from my home in Scottsdale, Arizona, to such places as the site of the world's tallest thermometer (135 feet, in Baker, California) or state park campgrounds offering reduced rates for tent sites because of recent bear attacks.

* * *

The first stories, because all stories begin with ones that came before, are of my father, who ran away from home at an even earlier age than I did and went to sea, during World War II, and by the time he was seventeen had circled the globe. Then he took to the air and spent thirty years flying for Pan American Airways. But he loved to travel by any means. And it was on a meandering family road trip from New York to San Francisco, when I was seven, and the first of my two sisters was four, that I became aware that no matter where our journeys brought us, he always had a story to tell about it. The story was always dramatic and always featured him in some heroic role.

In Pennsylvania, near the birthplace of Daniel Boone, my father pointed out where he'd helped the great woodsman—who was lost at the time—find his way over the Appalachian Mountains to what was then the American Frontier. As we crossed Indiana, he explained that when he'd come that way before, the journey had been much more arduous because he'd been on foot, lugging a burlap sack for Johnny Appleseed. And as we looked out upon the Mississippi River, he remembered the hours he'd spent studying its waters from the pilothouse of a paddlewheel steamboat before finally coming up with a name Samuel Clemens was pleased to call himself.

The story that made the most lasting impression, though, was one he told us in Colorado as our Nash Rambler station wagon negotiated the 156 hairpin turns in the twelve miles of road that climbs Pikes Peak, the often-snow-covered mountain whose views, looking out toward the Great Plains, inspired the lyrics for "America the Beautiful."

"It should have been called Payne's Peak, after us," my father said of the mountain. "And it would have been, too, if old Colonel Pike hadn't worn himself out trying to climb it."

They weren't even halfway up, my father claimed, before Pike lagged so far behind that my father had to come back down, get behind him, and push, giving the winded soldier the credit, and the glory, for being first to the top.

"And the story gets worse, children," said my mother, her long red hair billowing around her as she turned toward us from the front passenger seat of the Rambler.

In reality, she said, reading from a tourist brochure she'd picked up in Colorado Springs earlier that day, *Lieutenant* Zebulon Pike, a U.S. army officer who had been tasked with exploring part of what is now southeastern Colorado, never reached the summit of the peak, which he attempted to climb in 1806, at the age of twenty-six.

"And that means, I am afraid, that your father was pushing the wrong man."

My father remained silent long enough for me to become aware of the sound of our tires crunching in the summer snow that clung to the road's unpaved surface.

"I guess that explains," he finally said, "why the fellow was dressed like an Indian."

Every good travel tale, my parents were helping me begin to understand, requires a hero and a fact-checker.

* * *

As for my first solo journey, when I was fifteen, I embarked on it not because of any painful childhood experience. I was just continuing a family history of itinerancy, which compelled me to see all the states we had not visited during our earlier travels. There were thirteen, not counting Hawaii and Alaska, and I saw them all. Then, at the end of the summer, I hitchhiked back to Florida, where my parents were so glad to see me that I was able to negotiate the terms of my grounding down from all the rest of high school to just through the eleventh grade.

I wrote a book about that journey, four hundred double-spaced pages, pecked out on the family typewriter at a thousand words a day. I finished the first draft while working on it in the afternoons after school, in the eleventh grade, when I would have been out playing baseball or riding motorbikes if I hadn't been grounded.

Then, I spent the next fifteen years editing and revising the manuscript. Until finally, I lost the entire thing when I had to leave it in the care of a woman who did not tell me, until inconveniently late, that she was married, to a husband on his way home, from prison.

Sometimes, I still think about that woman. And when I do, I am reminded of the importance of making a copy of everything you write and keeping it separate from the original.

* * *

People who hear the story of my first solo journey often argue that when I was fifteen, a kid could have an adventure like mine with far less risk than one could today. They insist that the times were more innocent, with less likelihood of bad things happening. But I don't think the times were more innocent, just more unreported.

None of the people who gave me a ride that first summer were what you would call normal. They all wanted something: gas money, to make a better Christian of me, the chance to tell someone that the vehicle we were riding in across the cornfields of Nebraska, at a hundred miles an hour, was stolen.

Of all the rides I got, only one, somewhere south of Fort Smith, Arkansas, was from what at first seemed to be an ordinary family—a young couple and their baby. And the couple, it turned out, wanted to give me the baby.

"I can tell you'd make a good parent," the woman said, pausing as if to reconsider before adding, "Better than us, anyway."

I parted ways with that family by bolting from the car at the first place we stopped for gas. And I was relieved when all that my next ride wanted was to show me photos of his wife, naked.

Later, heading back East, I was targeted on a rural road outside Minneapolis by a car full of drive-by shooters. Fortunately, though, at that point in their careers, they had managed to progress no further than BB guns. When I didn't react to the stinging pellets but just kept walking, they pulled up alongside me, matching my pace, and we talked for a while. And like me, they were just guys, with no idea of what was coming.

"You heard about Vietnam?" one of them asked. "Soon as we can, we want to get over there, take care of some of them Viet Cong."

Instead of making me fear travel, though, my experiences that summer convinced me I wanted to do more of it. They convinced me that I delighted in listening to the stories of strangers in far places. That's why, the following summer, when I was sixteen, I was gone again.

* * *

My parents, demonstrating what some people might call a monumental lack of judgment, had allowed me to fly by myself from Miami to Mexico City for a summer-vacation visit with a school friend's family. After a day with the family, I departed, unannounced, on a 1,500-mile bus trip that ended in Panama City, Panama.

Getting by on my high school Spanish, which was easy enough if you went to high school in Miami, I followed the Pan

American Highway for almost the length of Central America.

Sometimes, the road took me through dusty towns where people lived in rooms separated from unpaved streets only by a blanket hanging in a doorway. Sometimes, it traversed rolling landscapes of banana plantations, green and yellow in the tropical sunlight. And sometimes, it forced its way over washed-out mountain passes we had to push boulders off of so the bus could squeeze by.

At meal stops, I ate parts of chickens I could not identify. And at border crossings, I wondered about the lives of soldiers who were so young, some younger than me, even, that the rifles they slung over their shoulders dragged on the ground behind them.

In Guatemala City, I was approached by a man who wanted to shine my shoes for ten centavos, or about a dime. But after he determined that I was alone, he claimed he had a special ingredient that would keep the shoes shiny forever but would cost me a hundred centavos.

I would have paid him because it seemed like a reasonable price, including as it did the opportunity to hear yet another stranger's story. But a policeman who happened along, and threatened to beat the man with a club, disagreed.

In Tegucigalpa, Honduras, as I waited at a bus station where another traveler had assured me I would have my pockets picked, an old lady rubbed the blond hair on my forearms, cackled, "Rubio bonito," and relieved my pockets of the coins I had budgeted for her.

For three days through Nicaragua and Costa Rica, I sat on a bus across from a young woman, a girl, really, not that much older than me, dressed all in black and looking pretty in her tears. Sometimes we talked, and sometimes she smiled. Until finally, in a place where the road ran along the spine of a mountain, she got off the bus and, looking down into a ravine whose depths were concealed by mist, made the sign of the cross.

Her husband and the truck he had been driving, I pieced together from the whispers, were still somewhere down in the ravine. After a few minutes, the young woman picked up her small traveling bag and crossed the road to where she apparently intended to wait for the next bus heading north. And I was left wondering, for the rest of my life, what it would have been like to get off the bus and go with her.

* * *

In Panama City, I heard that not much farther south, the road was impassably broken by the Darien Gap, a miasmal swamp across which no wheeled vehicle could travel. So, after some thought of trying to cross the Gap on foot, I called my parents and asked if they would send me the money for an air ticket home. Being my parents, and, in my opinion, just about the best parents I could have had, they said they would.

A few days later, my flight was scheduled to leave in the evening. A tip of two U.S. quarters, delivered with a flourish to a hotel desk clerk when I paid my bill of five American dollars for two nights, elicited a suggestion from him for how I might want to spend an otherwise uncommitted afternoon.

"I think you no have enough money for a prostitute," the desk clerk said, rubbing his whiskered chin. "So, maybe is better you visit Isla Taboga."

The island, which I later learned had played a significant but little-known role in the career of the painter Paul Gauguin, lay just offshore of the city, twelve miles out in the Pacific. Hilly and green, it was a refuge from the heat of the mainland, the desk clerk told me, with a white sand beach, flowers everywhere, and places by the sea where you could eat fresh fish.

Because I had never been to an island, ending my journey with a visit to one appealed to me. Especially since the desk clerk said he could arrange a "special price" for the ferry, a price that was, I discovered only after boarding, a little more than twice what everyone else had paid.

The money was well spent, though, because at one of the places by the sea I fell into a conversation with an American man who walked with a limp he told me he'd gotten on an island in the Western Pacific when the brother of a local woman he'd found irresistibly attractive put a spear through his leg. He'd been on the island, he said, writing a story for a magazine. He was, he told me, a travel writer.

I looked out to where ships were entering and exiting the Panama Canal and imagined being aboard one of them, headed for Tahiti, or Fiji, or—although I wasn't sure which ocean it was in—what was then known as Ceylon.

Travel writer, I thought to myself. That sounds like the life for me.

2
Distant Music Only Some Can Hear

It took me a while to get there. The year after I finished the first draft of my solo travel narrative, I started college but dropped out, at the height of the Vietnam War, with plans to join the Army. I thought enlisting would allow me to see a part of the world that at the time was accessible to Americans only if you came armed. And it seemed that the experience might make a good book. Like *Catch-22*, except with dining and accommodation tips.

But the Army, at the height of the Vietnam War, didn't want me. For two days at the induction center in Jacksonville, Florida, I was tested and probed and tested some more. Mostly because of a knee I'd torn playing street football. Until finally, I was escorted out through the gates along with a guy who dressed like Jesus and was leading a sheep on a leash.

"It's not fair," the guy protested, with what might have been mock indignity, as the MP's closed the gates behind us. "Plenty of people kiss their dogs, and it doesn't keep *them* out of the Army."

* * *

At eighteen, I married a girl I'd met in college, and we lived for a while in Florida aboard a houseboat I'd designed myself and built in my parent's driveway with no help from anyone. Except, toward the end, a few neighbors who desperately wanted it gone.

Inspired by the Henry David Thoreau quote "If a man does not keep pace with his companions, perhaps it is because he hears a different drummer. Let him step to the music he hears, however measured or far away," I named the boat *Distant Music*.

The plan was that *Distant Music* would be our floating magic carpet. It would take us on long voyages, perhaps even through the South Pacific, to Tahiti. Along the way, I would write about our adventures. Unfortunately, the boat's shoebox-like shape turned out to be a design flaw that, in all but flat calm, made it manageable only when tied to a dock.

We were tied to a dock near Jupiter Inlet, just north of Palm Beach, Florida, when our daughter, Kristina, was born. Chronicling her early months afloat resulted in my first published story, in *Boating* magazine, for which I earned $75. I would come to recall the amount with amusement until, decades later, I started writing for the Internet.

Besides giving me an inflated view of my place in world literature, a result of the *Boating* story was that it caught the eye of a live-aboard neighbor at the dock who was an editor at *The Palm Beach Post*. *The Post* was looking for a newsroom clerk, and with his help, I got the job. It was a lowly position, but one that soon had family and friends growing weary of hearing me refer to myself as a newspaperman.

Mostly, in those antediluvian days before computers, my function was to take dictation over the phone from reporters who called in their stories. But I was also encouraged to write. And I sometimes wish I'd stayed longer because I think that the editors at *The Post*—with their edict that no lede (as we newspapermen spelled the term for the introductory part of a story) could be more than thirty words—were well on their way to stamping out my tendency toward clauses that wander for often challenging distances.

I left *The Post* because a man willing to think inside the box made us an unexpectedly good offer for *Distant Music*, allowing me to return to college, at the University of South Florida, in Tampa, to study journalism. After graduating, I got a job with the now-defunct *Tampa Times* as the Outdoors Writer. In part, I believe, because I mentioned on my resume that I had been a boat builder.

Bass fishing, duck hunting, deer hunting with a bow and arrow: I had to do it all for *The Times*, much too often wearing camouflage. Once, I was almost drummed out of a hunting camp for hesitating to eat armadillo meat. And once, I was deaf for three days after a hunter sitting next to me in the back seat of a Volkswagen van accidentally fired his black-powder rifle through the roof.

At *The Times*, drawn to the waters of Tampa Bay and the Gulf of Mexico and remembering stories my father used to tell about his days at sea, I started writing about the sport of sailing. And soon enough, by paying as little attention as possible to the traditional outdoor sports and introducing *The Times* readers to a level of sailing coverage hardly matched by even Rhode Island's *The Providence Journal* during an America's Cup year, I was working elsewhere.

Eventually, following a pretty good run as a freelancer specializing in anything to do with boats, including doing work for *The New York Times*, I ended up as an editor at *Sail* magazine, in Boston, which most people in my circle considered the job of a lifetime, and where I lasted for less than a year.

* * *

What doomed me at *Sail* was an exchange I witnessed one morning in front of our office, at Commercial Wharf, on Boston Harbor. The exchange was between one of our freelance writers and a Boston policeman, who was mounted on a horse.

The writer, Tristan Jones, was a consummate storyteller who made no effort to separate the facts of his life from the fiction. He had been writing magazine pieces about an offbeat adventure in which he attempted to set a "vertical sailing record" by launching a boat first into the Dead Sea, whose surface sits at about 1,300 feet below sea level, and then hauling the boat up to the world's highest navigable body of water, South America's Lake Titicaca, at about 12,500 feet.

From the magazine stories, Tristan had just put together a book, *The Incredible Voyage*, which among the sailing crowd would become a bestseller and was the first of more than a dozen he wrote, all in a similar hard-to-believe but always entertaining vein.

That morning, before going up to the office, on the second floor of what had once been a mercantile warehouse, I was on my way into a convenience store when I saw Tristan standing beside a flatbed truck double-parked on busy Atlantic Avenue. On the back of the truck was a boat, its name, *Sea Dart*, boldly painted on the side, aboard which he'd supposedly done the sailing adventure and was now hauling around the country for a book tour. (Actually, there had been two boats, and I'm not sure if he ever did sail either of them in the Dead Sea. But never mind.)

The policeman, his horse towering over Tristan, was red-faced with rage, and the horse, doing a sidestepping jig, appeared to be in none-too-serene a state itself.

About ten minutes later, when I came out of the convenience store, Tristan was nowhere to be seen. The truck was still there, though, and the policeman, still mounted on his now-quiescent horse, was thumbing through what was no doubt an autographed copy of *The Incredible Voyage*.

That's what my life is supposed to be like, I thought: Adventures in far places and creating words about them powerful enough to ward off even parking tickets, even in Boston.

I went up to my desk, announced my resignation with a note I left in my typewriter, and, without talking to anyone, walked out the door. At home, I made a similarly brief announcement, essentially leaving my wife a single mother of, by then, three children, and leaving me, for the rest of my life, to make my intended reader anyone who might wonder if they, too, in the pursuit of a goal, could abandon good jobs, great marriages, and small children.

3
Introducing the Maldives

Over the next few years, in search of stories to write, I pursued a series of sailing adventures. On a voyage from New York to Plymouth, England, I was part of a four-man team that tried (but, because of light winds, failed) to break the transatlantic speed record under sail. Cruising the coast of Ireland, I navigated through thick fog by listening, as the Irish claimed they did, for dogs barking along the shore. A barking-dog navigator was the term for a skilled practitioner of the art, which I never became. And in an offshore sailing race from Florida to Mexico, I served as the cook for an otherwise all-female crew of eight who delighted in humiliating me at every opportunity. The most egregious of their cruelties occurred on a day when a Coast Guard patrol plane flying low overhead caused them to rip off their tops, wave them in the air, and shout, "It's the Coast Guard. It's men."

I wrote about most of my adventures as a freelancer for *Sail*, where my abrupt departure from the office had generated surprisingly little ill will.

I was fortunate during those years because *Sail's* editor, Keith Taylor, and its managing editor, Patience Wales, seemed happy enough to let me head off, with only the vaguest of assignments and a little bit of expense money, in any direction I could convince them might prove interesting to readers. The only exception was when I proposed that the magazine buy me a boat, designed and built by anyone but me, capable of sailing to Tahiti.

In a roundabout way, my association with Patience made it possible for me to take what would prove to be the next, and arguably most significant, step in my travel writing life, which was to break into the pages of *Condé Nast Traveler*.

In 1987, Patience took a year's leave of absence from *Sail* with plans to circle the globe aboard her 54-foot boat, *Boston Light*. Upon her departure, some stay-behinds had speculated and perhaps hoped, as some stay-behinds always will, that when her leave ended, she might not get her old job back. Instead, she was returning to become the new editor-in-chief.

There was a problem, though. *Boston Light* was still out in the Indian Ocean, in The Maldives, only halfway through its circumnavigation. So, Patience asked if I would like to join her husband, Knowles Pittman, and their friend Kenneth Wunderlich in sailing the boat across the Indian Ocean and through the Suez Canal into the Mediterranean, where someone else would take my place. It was a leg of the voyage available, I am sure, because of the concern among other potential crewmembers about possible confrontation in the Gulf of Aden and the Red Sea with rocket-launcher-armed pirates looking for some way to temper their disappointment in not having bagged an infidel oil tanker.

Although I immediately volunteered, there was a concern for me, too. After my first wife and I split up for good, and following a relationship with a British woman that ended tragically, for me, when she married the captain of the boat we were crewing aboard during a passage across the Pacific, I'd met a woman in Boston who I was now living with. And despite her many fine qualities, an enthusiasm for me leaving her behind to go sailing in pirate-infested waters on the other side of the world was not among them.

But you negotiate these things. You talk about how good it could be for your career. You float the idea that writing about the places you will be visiting is a way to move on from special-interest publications such as *Sail*, which, no matter how good they've been to you, are by their nature limited in the exposure they can generate and the money they can pay.

You talk about the more general-interest travel magazines, with their broader circulations and higher pay (a relative comparison, admittedly). And you point out the success of travel writers such as Paul Theroux and Bill Bryson and—in those days—William Least Heat Moon.

And when all that fails, you suggest, despite what you'd think experience might have taught you, that when you get back, perhaps the two of you should discuss marriage.

* * *

Leaving Boston on a snowy day in March, I flew via San Francisco and Singapore to Male, the capital of The Maldives, where, above a moonlit sea, filled to the horizon by a dark scattering of islands, my Singapore Airlines 747 descended toward a runway that looked much too much for my taste like the deck of an aircraft carrier.

My seatmate, a New Zealander who had a contract to build fuel-storage tanks for the native fishermen, didn't seem a bit concerned. At least that's what I assumed by the coolness with which he slipped an airline copy of *Time* magazine into his carry-on bag. My only consoling thought—although not that consoling—was that one way or another I was seconds away from achieving a goal worthy of even the most passport-stamped traveler.

About as far from home as an American could get without joining the space program, and nowhere near the Pacific, I was about to arrive at an isolated island group where the word atoll comes from. Meaning a ring of islands or coral reefs, the word is derived from the Maldivian language, Divehi, which is spoken almost nowhere else on earth except in a few New York City taxicabs.

Without incident, though, we touched down about midnight, and I discovered, thanks to the New Zealander, that if Maldivian customs officials find anything in your bags resembling pornography (which, as representatives of a Muslim nation, they considered to be everything that shows skin above the ankles) everyone else's bags get only a cursory inspection because the officials will be preoccupied with trying to take a better look at the offending material—in this case an ad in the airline copy of *Time*.

Which was fine with me because I had a duffel bag full of replacements for various odd-looking boat parts, many of them electronic, which Patience had arranged for me to bring out to Knowles and Kenneth. And I knew that customs officials often looked upon that kind of stuff as an opportunity to charge a substantial import duty or, more often, an only slightly less substantial bribe.

Because of the attention being paid to the New Zealander, though, I sailed right through inspection and found Kenneth and Knowles waiting just outside the customs exit. Where, no doubt because they'd been away from home for more than a year, they seemed far more interested in the newspapers I brought with me than in how my journey had gone.

"My plane was late out of Boston because of a snowstorm," I said as I handed them a half dozen well-traveled *Boston Globes*. "And by the time I got to Singapore, they had given away my room at Raffles. But I had a reservation, so they had to find something for me. Which is how I ended up with the honeymoon suite. It was funny because the bellman kept looking down the hallway and asking if another person was coming."

To which Kenneth responded, "Where's the Sunday Sports section?"

* * *

The twenty-six coral atolls that make up the Indian Ocean nation officially known as the Republic of Maldives have been described by the Norwegian explorer Thor Heyerdahl, of *Kon-Tiki* fame, as "even more beautiful than any of the coral atolls in Polynesia." And when I arrived in 1988, it was a beauty only slowly being discovered by collectors of exotic destinations. Not many of them, but enough so that the Maldives was becoming a nation conflicted.

On the one hand, because a majority of the Maldivian population were Koran-reading, alcohol-shunning, five-times-a-day-praying Muslims whose professed ideas of proper conduct would have made Queen Victoria seem like a pole dancer, the country was trying to protect itself from what it saw as the socially polluting influence of outsiders. On the other hand, many Maldivians wanted to benefit financially from the allure their country's natural beauty had for those outsiders.

The compromise was to informally divide the country into three zones:

There was the island city of Male, where the locals, some twenty-five percent of the Maldivian population, had so learned to coexist with outsiders that the drivers of the water taxis plying back and forth between the town and the resort islands prepared for emergencies by equipping their boats with prayer mats for the Muslims and life jackets for the infidels.

Next, there were the local islands, about 200 of them, where the rest of the native population lived and where outsiders were discouraged—but not necessarily prohibited, as I was to discover—from visiting.

Then, there were the tourist-only islands, a dozen or so of them from among the thousand that would have otherwise been uninhabited. They were staffed entirely by non-Maldivians. And tourists staying on them were permitted to behave pretty much as tourists do everywhere, even to drinking alcohol and, as often goes hand in hand with it at beach resorts, appearing in public in various stages of undress.

Every time I went to Male, its shop-lined streets were always busy, always hectic. The favorite shop for most visitors—not because of the goods but because it was air-conditioned—was the duty-free store on Orchid Magu Street. My favorites, though, were the local places, where you could buy everything from shark jaws to exotic spices in hundred-pound sacks.

Most hectic of all was Marine Drive, on the Male waterfront. During daylight hours, a trickle of tourists tramped it, some from a Russian cruise ship anchored in the lagoon. Mixed with them were men with pull carts, men with wheelbarrows, and men with strong backs, who were carrying bananas, stacks of driftwood, cases of motor oil, and sacks of rice or spices that they had offloaded from the small trading craft jammed along the seawall.

Tourists and laborers alike were dodging trucks, cars, and motorbikes, which, because of some municipal improvements underway in the middle of the drive, were having no easy time of it themselves.

On occasion, when the breeze would give wing to the fragrances of the East, I would become aware that Marine Drive smelled like the college dorm I briefly resided in during the incense-burning days of the 1960s. On occasion, too, the cacophony of tongues would be overpowered by the wailing of loudspeakers calling the faithful to prayer at the Islamic Center mosque, whose giant dome of gold-anodized aluminum dominated the Male skyline.

* * *

By contrast, the local islands, or so I assumed from the one I visited, were as serene as they had probably been for millennia.

I'd met a European expat who talked me into bankrolling a fishing expedition, which meant I paid for the boat fuel. But after a few luckless hours of trolling along the reefs, we went ashore, as had been part of the bargain, to a local island he knew. There, he introduced me to the proprietor of a packing-crate-size, cement-and-coral, tin-roofed building with the word HOTEL written on it in English but that turned out to be a one-table eatery that served the best breakfast I had during my entire Maldives stay.

"Have whatever you want. It's on me," the expat said, as the proprietor, who seemed to be gossiping with him in Divehi, loaded down the table with saucer-size dishes of hard-boiled eggs, various fish, chicken and vegetable rolls, and the kinds of sticky-sweet desserts that were becoming socially acceptable only in Third World nations where the concept of cutting down on calories did not yet have relevance.

At the end of the meal, the proprietor tallied our bill by counting the number of empty saucers. Including drinks and tip (we'd splurged and had Cokes) the bill came to about three dollars.

After breakfast, I walked the length of the island's one street. It was about a hundred yards long, made of sand, and lined with palm trees and neat, well-spaced one-room houses whose windows and doors were open to the monsoon breeze. No one else was on the street, and although I could hear and see people in most of the houses, no one seemed to show the slightest interest in me. The exception was a yard full of brown-eyed children, who I got to giggle for my camera by doing an impersonation of a chicken that doesn't yet realize it will not remain a family member forever.

* * *

The tourist islands, each with one resort, were as idyllic as any I had ever seen. The islands' only drawback was that, because of the resorts, there sometimes seemed to be too many people around. The ideal population for a perfect tropical isle is, in my opinion, no larger than the Swiss Family Robinson, which, if you count the English girl, the orphan monkey, and the pet jackal, is nine.

Still, a compensation for the overcrowding was that a walk along the beach often made it possible to keep an eye on the progress of the German and Italian women who were learning to windsurf, topless.

The first of the tourist islands to be developed, Kurumba, a short boat ride from the airport, was built in 1972. The story was that a few years earlier, an Italian tour operator just happened to stumble on the Maldives and immediately saw their potential as an exotic destination for winter-weary Europeans. That same year, he returned with a planeload of Italian travel writers.

The travel writers stayed on Kurumba and went home to report—as travel writers on an all-expenses-paid press trip are often inclined to do anyway—that they had discovered paradise.

Yet while by the late 1980s, the resorts were becoming an "in" place for Europeans who collected exotic destinations, the Maldives remained virtually undiscovered by Americans.

"Perhaps it is because few people in America know where we are," Abdul Shakoor Ahmed, the deputy director of tourism, told me one morning when I wandered into his office unannounced. "But then, few people anywhere know where we are."

The deputy director, who wore a tie and admitted he wished he didn't have to, was being modest. There were all those Europeans. Yet where he saw a challenge, I saw the proverbial opportunity.

Although I had no assignment, had not queried anyone, had never even had a story appear in a bona fide travel magazine, I planned to write a piece about an undiscovered paradise—undiscovered by Americans, at least. Maybe not the most original idea, true, but appealing enough so that I was able to get a story published that not only changed my life but also, I like to think, the lives of a nation.

I'm getting ahead of myself, but I returned to Boston not only knowing that I wanted to write a story about The Maldives but knowing, too, where I hoped to see it published. My goal was *Condé Nast Traveler*, a magazine that was then, and still is, considered one of the travel genre's best-paying, most prestigious, and hardest to break into.

What drew me to *Traveler* was that more than the other two magazines I most aspired to write for—*National Geographic* and *Travel & Leisure*—it seemed to let writers speak in their own voice. Of course, what would interest them in my voice was a question yet to be answered.

With a no-doubt necessary amount of naiveté and self-confidence, I looked at the list of editors on *Condé Nast Traveler's* masthead, picked one, Michael Shnayerson, because he had written something I liked, and sent him a query letter. The letter asserted that I had actually been to the Maldives, as had a considerable number of European jet setters but virtually no other Americans. It asserted that I had a track record as a newspaper journalist and magazine writer and editor, although neglecting to mention just how spotty that record was. And it included my anecdote about how my New Zealand seatmate slipped the Singapore Airlines copy of *Time* magazine into his briefcase.

To even my surprise, Michael responded not with the half-expected standard rejection letter but by telephoning me.

The first thing he asked, noting how close to the top of my query letter I had mentioned Singapore Airlines, was if I had paid for my airfare or gotten a freebie.

"Because our writers can accept no freebies," he said, making me feel as good as you might imagine that the letter I had written to Singapore Airlines, asking for a free ticket, had gone unanswered.

After I assured him that I had, of course, paid for the ticket myself and mentioned the airline only as a way of letting people know that, as remote as the Maldives were, getting there was not impossibly difficult, Michael said he could make me only one promise.

"If you write the story, on speculation, with no commitment on our part, I'll read it."

I did, he did, and *Condé Nast Traveler* bought it, running it as a cover story for their September 1989 issue.

That's how I became a writer and later a contributing editor for the magazine. It truly was no more difficult—not counting the years beforehand that I'd spent developing my writing and traveling skills—than coming up with an idea for a story powerful enough to change the lives of a nation.

And I think you could argue, given the influence of *Condé Nast Traveler*, and that there are now more than a hundred resorts in The Maldives, with many free-spending Americans among their guests, that my story did help do just that.

It certainly changed my life, giving me credentials that opened doors that might otherwise have remained closed. It's how I got into *Outside* magazine, for example, where the editor I first corresponded with seemed much less interested in what I might do for them than how he, too, might get into *Traveler*.

Before I could write the story, though, or even pitch the idea—in those days when almost no one had a laptop and e-mail hardly existed—I had to get home from half a world away

4

Stoned in Egypt, But Not in a Good Way

Despite the possibility of encountering pirates, *Boston Light*'s 2,200-mile non-stop passage across the Indian Ocean from the Maldives to the tiny North African nation of Djibouti turned out to be easy. For two weeks, we drifted along under sail. Or, when the breeze abandoned us altogether, we motored. We slept or imagined meals we could make if we had anything fresh. And we read books we would never have found time for ashore, such as *Reeds Nautical Almanac*, particularly its section on childbirth at sea.

Djibouti, on the Gulf of Aden, where Africa's Great Rift Valley touches the sea, was no Disney World. On the outskirts of Djibouti City, in whose harbor we anchored, I saw camps where some 20,000 Ethiopian refugees lived. Even downtown, you could see dirt, and you could see poverty. You could see tiny, emaciated children with their hands out. And you could see ingratiating con artists, such as a ten-year-old boy who, deducing from the absence of an ultra-short French-military-style haircut that I was American, greeted me in English with "America good, Russia bad." Then he asked for cigarettes. When I told him I had none, he walked away muttering, "Russia good, America bad."

But you could also see, perhaps while you were strolling past the market stalls along Place Mahmoud Harbi or coming out of a store with your daily supply of bottled water and still-warm French bread, Djiboutian women with such beautiful faces and gazelle-like grace that they would startle you. And you could see that even the swagger of the khaki-clad local police had a hard time standing up to a smile and the French version of "What's happening?"

For my first-ever newspaper travel story, which I sold unsolicited to *The Boston Globe*, I wrote about a tour I took into the desert surrounding Djibouti in the company of four young French sailors who were among the crew of a minesweeper that was part of a large French naval fleet based at Djibouti City.

The sailors and our guide spoke only a few words of English, and my French was pretty much limited to "Ça va?" But with signs all around us of volcanic activity so recent that the scene looked like a battlefield from which the smoke was still rising, you didn't need someone to explain that we were looking at how worlds are created.

Mostly, the young sailors reacted to the geological spectacle as if they were noisy schoolboys, which, until recently, they no doubt had been.

They pretended to throw each other into the steep-sided crater of a volcano that last erupted in 1978. They dared their companions to dash beneath a natural bridge of jagged black lava that already showed evidence of being shaken apart by Djibouti's frequent earthquakes. They ran across the crumbling salt flats of Lake Assal, which at 512 feet below sea level is the lowest point in Africa. And, as evidence that evolution is only a theory, they tried to light their cigarettes by holding them up to spumes of steam venting through a crack in the earth.

They were pleasant enough traveling companions, though, and at the end of the tour they presented me with a gift—a slab of salt they'd picked up at Lake Assal and forgotten, or so they claimed, to use at lunch.

* * *

Heading back to *Boston Light*, I was accosted on the street by two men waving worn-looking rifles and dressed in what appeared to be cast-off pieces of military uniforms. They demanded I pay a "fine" for an infraction they never could make clear to me, as they seemed to be speaking a French even more disjointed than mine.

Before it was over, the men had marched me at gunpoint to what turned out to be a local police station containing a single cell occupied by a frail, ragged-looking man who sat morosely on a blanket on the floor. However, his mood improved considerably when one of my captors unlocked the cell door and ordered him out. The accommodation, the policeman suggested through gestures, could easily be mine.

As interesting as it might have been to spend some time in a North African jail, I decided to pay the fine instead. And the amount the men exacted, about five dollars in Djiboutian francs, no doubt to be spent on khat, the euphoria-inducing drug much of the male population around the Horn of Africa is addicted to, proved well worth it. Because the next day, when I saw the two men on the street again, they grinned and gave me a thumbs-up signal.

And I felt I had friends in Djibouti.

* * *

In contrast to the lazy days on the Indian Ocean, our Red Sea passages, to Port Sudan, along the North African coast, then Port Suez, in Egypt, were among the most intense times I have ever spent on the water.

In part, the cause was difficulties we had expected: fierce headwinds, unlit oil platforms, and crowded shipping lanes.

And in part, it was the failure of *Boston Light*'s automated self-steering mechanism, meaning that because there were no ports we could put into along the physically and politically inhospitable coast, we had to hand steer the boat around the clock for 700 miles. Under the circumstances, that would have been bad enough. But making it worse, Kenneth came down with something, probably a recurrence of the malaria he'd first gotten in the Pacific, which kept him in his bunk for a good part of the time.

The work was exhausting, the kind of exhaustion that causes you to see ships' lights that turn out to be stars and not to see unlit oil platforms that turn out to be right on top of you. But I loved it, especially the feeling that you were about as close to the elements as you could get. And I think Kenneth and Knowles loved it, too. I remember one day in particular, with the wind howling and solid water washing over *Boston Light*'s crazily heeled deck, when I am sure they did.

Kenneth was out of his bunk and in the cockpit, steering, because we couldn't have done without him at that moment. Knowles, dressed in florescent yellow foul weather gear, was on the bow, wearing a safety harness so that he wouldn't be swept over the side as he wrestled with a sail we needed to haul down and replace with a smaller one. I was at the mast, working various sail controls and following an age-old dictum that every nautical chronicler knows well: One hand for yourself, and one for the ship, and one for the camera.

"Knowles," I shouted, "Smile."

He looked up and smiled, and, as I clicked away with my waterproof camera, was inundated by a wall of white water. From which it took him so long to reappear that I wondered if we were now going to be even more short-handed.

Knowles turned sixty-five that day, and we called the photo his sixty-fifth birthday portrait. It ran on the February 1990 cover of *Sail*, and among all the photos I have taken, it is a favorite, ranking high even when measured against the shots that would have been award-worthy had I remembered to take the lens cap off.

*   *   *

After the drama of the Red Sea, the Suez Canal was one long uneventful ditch. As far as I could see, its only value, other than shortening the sea route between the Arabian Peninsula and Europe by about 9,000 miles, was that it allowed me to become proficient at reading the mile-marker numbers posted in Arabic along the bank, mile after monotonous mile. I became so good at it that later, in Cairo, not a single taxi driver was able to tell me the meter read one thing when clearly it read something else.

The canal's monotony, however, was made up for in Port Said, at the Mediterranean end, when shortly after our arrival Kenneth, who sometimes had a slight problem with drink, sent me off with a taxi driver to pick up some supplies he'd ordered, neglecting to tell me that I was on a beer run.

It was Ramadan, the Muslim holy month, when during daylight hours Muslims are not supposed to eat, drink, smoke, engage in sex, or, as I was to learn all too well, unlock the doors of beer warehouses for infidels.

The taxi driver had exchanged some words, and money, with a warehouse guard. And they were just handing me, to my surprise, a case of beer, when a knot of veiled, black-garbed women stepped out of a door next to the warehouse.

Yelling and waving their arms, the women advanced toward us.

I've always argued that the wisest course any traveler can take when coming face to face with strangers whose intentions are not immediately welcoming is to smile and say hello in their language, which communicates that despite your ignorance of so many things, you are at least human.

So that's what I did. "As-salamu alaykum," I said. "Peace be upon you."

And that's when the women began throwing stones.

As the taxi rocketed backward out of the alley, its wheels screeching and kicking up dust, I believe the driver and I were both at the wheel.

* * *

Bruised, but not debilitatingly so, I left *Boston Light* in Port Said but spent another few weeks in Egypt. I saw the pyramids and the tomb of King Tut. I had the required photo taken of me on a camel, cruised the Nile aboard a river steamer, and climbed Mount Sinai in the pre-dawn dark, arriving at the summit in time to watch the sunrise.

I wrote about my first Sinai climb for the now-departed *Travel-Holiday* magazine, recommending to its readers that if the spirit of their surroundings prompted climbers to attempt explaining the unexplainable, they might want to see if they could determine why the restaurant at the tourist hotel at the base of the mountain sometimes played Christmas music all through the evening meal—apparently regardless of the season.

My favorite experience in Egypt, though, which I would eventually write about for a column I used to do for *iExplore.com*, was riding a local bus across the Sinai Desert.

Making friends with the locals when traveling in foreign countries, as long as you are not part of an invading army or trying to buy beer on Ramadan, is usually relatively easy. You learn a word or two of their language—not enough to converse, but, as I've said, just to reassure them that you are not some kind of alien being. You smile often, and if understanding has progressed to that level, you agree with any shortcomings they may have observed in whoever your national leader is at the time.

But keeping friends in foreign countries can be much trickier, as I was reminded while riding that local bus through the Sinai.

Western visitors do not often ride Egyptian buses, perhaps with good reason. The temperature was well over a hundred degrees the morning we set out on an all-day journey to St. Catherine's Monastery, near Mount Sinai, on a bus with no air-conditioning. There were probably eighty passengers on the bus, which had seats for forty-four. Yet, for the first hour, the seat next to mine remained empty. Out of politeness, fear, disdain, or, most likely, a suspicion of how long it had been since I'd washed my clothes, no one wanted to sit next to me.

Finally, a young male, perhaps braver than the rest or suffering from a head cold, sat down, making sure as he did so not to acknowledge my existence. When he seemed settled in, I pulled out my water bottle and offered it to him. The gesture startled him, but he took a drink. A few minutes later, he unwrapped an oiled-paper parcel and offered me a piece of what looked like a family-size Fig Newton. After taking a bite, I smiled, he smiled, and we were buddies.

Soon, it seemed that all the other passengers had managed to circulate past our seats, sometimes more than once, to get a look at me. My seatmate spoke no English, and my Arabic, other than knowing the written numbers, did not go much beyond translations of "Hello, Thank you," and "A room farther from the gunfire, please." But as he spoke to each passerby, I could tell that he was saying something like, "This guy's all right. We go way back."

I smiled at them all and usually got a smile in return, the only exceptions being the few women on the bus and the men I took to be their guardians.

Then, somewhere in the middle of the desert, the bus came

to a stop, and I looked out the window to see that we were at a military checkpoint. I turned to my seatmate to see if I could tell from his demeanor what the checkpoint might mean and discovered that the seat next to mine was again empty.

A soldier climbed onto the bus and, seeing me, the only Westerner aboard, walked slowly down the aisle to my seat. "Passport," he said, and I realized, as I reached down into the front of my pants to pull out the required document, that eighty pairs of eyes were focused on my crotch. The soldier flipped through the passport, handed it back without comment, and, on his way out, signaled to the driver that we could go.

The checkpoint wasn't out of sight behind us before my seatmate was back. He smiled, gave me a thumb's up, and resumed filling in the other passengers on the many details of my life's story.

And I felt I had friends in Egypt.

5
The Not So Rapido to Puerto Montt

A year elapsed between *Condé Nast Traveler* buying my first story and running it. During that time, I felt so encouraged that I wrote dozens of travel pieces, many of them published, primarily by newspapers. In addition to *The Boston Globe*, the papers, big and small, ranged from the *Los Angeles Times* to the *Maine Sunday Telegram*, and, happily, because I aspired to an international audience, Canada's *Kitchener-Waterloo Record*.

I wrote on everything from a wedding I had witnessed at a subway station in Singapore to a road trip to Graceland for what would have been Elvis Presley's birthday. My most successful story, though, whose setting I could have walked to from Boston, detailed where then-president George H. W. Bush shopped and dined out when he was at his family's summer compound in Kennebunkport, Maine.

The Kennebunkport story ran in fifteen or sixteen papers, including the *Miami Herald*, *The Providence Journal*, and *The Denver Post*, with revelations that were apparently newsworthy across the nation. It revealed, for instance, that you didn't have to tip much at Mabel's Lobster Claw Restaurant to leave more than the president did when he visited. And it revealed that if you were drawn to fast action, you could ask to see a remote-control model speedboat like the one Bush bought for himself, although claiming it was for his grandson, when he visited the Golden Goose Toy Shop.

You learned that at a gift shop called "What's in Store," you could buy a pair of bedroom slippers with a puppet-size likeness of the president sitting astride one foot and Barbara Bush, wearing her signature pearls, sitting astride the other.

You knew that at all but the few art galleries and studios whose proprietors would show you to the door for even suggesting that they might be influenced by what the general public wanted, you could find that Walker's Point, site of the Bush compound, was a popular subject for drawings, watercolors, and oil paintings.

And you knew that even more popular in many shops were the "kinder, gentler" George Bush masks on which were printed a warning that they were not to be worn by small children or vice-president Dan Quayle.

The pay for those stories might be $150, or $70, or $40 per paper. But because I could submit them to as many papers as I liked, as long as they didn't have competing circulations, it added up. And it allowed me, without qualification, to call myself a travel writer.

* * *

In August 1988, three months after I returned from the Maldives, I got married for the second time. Not long after that, again testing the boundaries of my new bride's enthusiasm, I left on a journey from which there was some possibility I might go missing.

The journey, meant to take six weeks, was to South America. For a little magazine called *The International Railway Traveler*, it began with a train trip from Santiago, Chile, south for 650 miles to the end of the line at Puerto Montt. Or at least it was the end of the line in those days. Now, indicative of South American train travel in general, I don't think it runs at all.

Standing in Santiago's station, I remember thinking that the Supersalon train to Conception (which I am not sure runs now either) looked magnificent. Each car was emblazoned with bold, ultra-modern graphics, and at each door, a female attendant, as lovely as one would expect in a country full of lovely women, stood on a cordoned-off patch of red carpet to welcome passengers aboard and help them find their seats.

That, however, was not my train.

My train, the Rapido to Puerto Montt, looked like the weary long-distance traveler it was. There were no fancy color graphics and no lovely attendants. In their place were worn-out cars I suspected would be so rough riding that not even Paul Theroux would have been able to take notes while aboard them. On some of the cars, the windows betrayed evidence of a sport I would come to recognize as popular in Latin American neighborhoods bereft of other forms of entertainment: pelting the trains with rocks.

Late in the afternoon, we pulled out of the station right on time, generally a rare event in South America but not so rare in Chile, a country enormously influenced by a small but well-placed segment of its citizenry of German stock, many of them having arrived shortly after World War II, for reasons they kept to themselves.

In the dining car, which was almost empty, I shared a table with one of those Germans, who said he had lived in Chile for nearly forty-five years.

"When I first arrived, as a young man, I wished to learn English along with Spanish. But there were few English speakers here then," he said. "So, every Saturday, I would go to the cinema and watch American cowboy movies."

But as a language tool, he said, the movies had their limitations. It was not that often, for example, that you could bring a conversation around to "This town ain't big enough for the two of us, stranger."

After a night in a reclining seat, lullabied by the clacking of train wheels against rails and the occasional gunfire-like crack of rocks against windows, I awoke to find the air growing colder and the scenery growing more spectacular. We were in the Lake District, a land of rolling, golden farms, sky-blue lakes, and snow-capped volcanoes, through which a publication called *The Walking Magazine* had assigned me to travel afoot.

Alighting at Puerto Montt, I followed a course that took me through an alpine landscape along unpaved, pebbly roads where, at most, I'd encounter two or three vehicles a day, one of them perhaps pulled by a horse or an ox. Often, wherever I went, only Spanish was spoken. But it didn't matter. I knew enough and had no trouble getting by with hardly more than the Spanish for, "Hello," "Goodbye," and, "That's a fine-looking cow you have."

It was a welcoming landscape. In all the time I walked, the only person who didn't return my smile was a man driving a horse cart. Significantly, perhaps, the cart appeared to have no springs.

Although the walk was highlighted by a climb nearly to the snowline of a volcano that could have won a Mt. Fuji look-alike contest, the adventure was not of heroic proportions. Most nights, I paid for my lodging with a credit card, and on a dirt road on the way up the volcano, I was overtaken by an ice-cream truck.

My choice of lodgings, including one inn with a row of outboard motors clamped to the reception desk, was plentiful because the Chileans, who as a population were relatively well off and who liked to travel within their own country, all took their vacations at the height of the summer, which in the Southern Hemisphere is January and February. When I arrived at the end of March, I found that I was often the only guest in places that had most likely been booked solid just several weeks earlier.

That was a drawback only once, at the Hotel Haase, in

the lakeside village of Puerto Octay, where Mrs. Haase, an ancient but energetic German woman, apparently saw me as an opportunity to empty her kitchen of everything left over from the summer season.

"No, no," she said as, near to bursting, I struggled to my feet from the breakfast table. "First, you will eat more cake."

* * *

I spent most of the train ride back to Santiago talking to a California woman who, by profession, was a firefighter. Having spent a month working with her Chilean counterparts on the forested slopes of the Andes, she was on her way to Mendoza, Argentina, to climb Mount Aconcagua, which, at 22,841 feet, is the highest mountain in the western and southern hemispheres.

"Want to come?" she asked.

It wasn't a technical climb, she reassured me, just a tough uphill walk with some risk of altitude sickness and, if the weather caught you out, hypothermia.

I thought about it seriously but declined, telling myself that I didn't have suitable clothing, and, perhaps of more concern, the idea might not be met with approval at home.

I left the train feeling more like a responsible spouse than I could ever before remember, a feeling that lasted for about an hour. That's when I learned I might be able to visit, far out in the Pacific, the island where, in the early 1700s, the real-life model for Robinson Crusoe had been marooned. Except, because of the weather, I might be marooned there myself, perhaps until the following spring, six months away.

And there might be no way to let my new wife know.

6
Waving Goodbye from Robinson Crusoe's Island

In Daniel Defoe's 1791 novel, *Robinson Crusoe*, the hero is a shipwrecked sailor who lives for twenty-eight years on a desert island located somewhere in the Atlantic off the Orinoco River, where he is eventually able to afford live-in help in the form of the lapsed cannibal Friday. But the real-life model for Crusoe, Alexander Selkirk, had been stranded in the Pacific, for four years and four months, on one of the islands of the Juan Fernández archipelago, far off the Chilean coast.

Either through a lack of imagination or because he had a sense of humor, the Spanish navigator Juan Fernández, who discovered the archipelago in 1574, named Selkirk's island Más a Tierra, meaning "closer to land." The land was the South American continent, 400 miles away. The name allowed Más a Tierra to be differentiated from the other main island of the group, Más Afuera, or "farther out," which lay a hundred miles to the west, deeper into the Pacific.

Small, under-populated, remote, and hard to get to, with green valleys and a gentle climate, Selkirk's island seemed to me, as it eventually would to Selkirk, the embodiment of Eden. Except that instead of Eve—and I am not making a value judgment—there were goats.

One of the reasons I had gone to Chile to do the train story and walk the Lake District was in the hope that I could also find a way to visit Selkirk's island, which all inquiry I did before leaving home, and in the few days I was in Santiago before heading south, suggested I would not be able to.

The problem was that the island, lying on the other side of the barrier-like Humboldt Current, which originates in Antarctica and remains so cold for so long that it allows penguins to feel at home in the Galapagos, has an approach made unpredictable by weather.

During the Southern Hemisphere summer, from November through March, the climate was a delight, sources said. But after that, clouds might blanket the island for days or weeks at a time. And because electronic communication with the mainland was almost non-existent, the small, twin-engine prop planes that ventured the three hours out there might not know until they arrived that cloud cover would make it necessary for them to turn around and fly back without landing.

By early April, when I was hoping to go, regularly scheduled flights had ended for the season. Still, I remained optimistic enough that I'd left almost a week open from when I returned from the Lake District until I was scheduled to fly home. So, when I was walking from the train station, looking for a hotel, and passed a travel agency that had a sign in the window offering flights to Isla Robinson Crusoe, I went in to inquire.

"Is no more for the season, I think," a woman at the agency told me. "But let me ask."

For twenty minutes, she was on the phone with someone at Aereos Isla Robinson Crusoe. She spent half of it asking about the family of the person on the other end. And half peppering her responses with the words "Norte Americano." As if that were answer enough to whatever questions were being put to her.

As she had thought, the season was over. But of possible interest to me, she said, was that a film crew from a Chilean television station was flying out to the island that day on a chartered plane. And they had so much equipment that the airline was arranging a second flight to carry the excess baggage.

There would be room on the second flight for me, she said, for $250 round trip. But only if I understood that the weather could strand me out there for a very long time. And I had to be at the airport in an hour, with a maximum ten kilos, or twenty-two pounds, of luggage.

"Could I leave a bag with you?" I asked her.

"Of course."

Knowing that there would be no way to reach my wife while I was on the island, I tried to call home to let her know my plans. But I couldn't get her, and this was before even answering machines. So, I went out to the airport feeling guilty that she might have to endure half a year of not knowing what had happened to her new husband.

However, I did not feel guilty enough to keep from squeezing in among a pile of camera gear when the second plane took off, headed for what would prove to be the setting for my second *Condé Nast Traveler* story. (And, if successful, Michael Shnayerson assured me, the last one I'd have to do on speculation.)

* * *

Desert red and barren on one side, green and cloud-topped on the other, Crusoe's island had a remoteness, a rugged topography, and a mild climate that had long made it a paradise for rare plants and for botanists working on their doctoral theses. The rarity and fragility of its plant life were why the entire archipelago, which Chile claims, had been declared a national park in 1935 and an internationally designated biosphere reserve in 1977.

As early as the 1920s, several passenger ships a year anchored at the island, giving rise to a practice, thankfully abandoned by the time I arrived, of its few residents dressing up in Crusoe-like goatskin ensembles at the first sign of tourists.

In 1966, Más a Tierra, Selkirk's island, was officially renamed Isla Robinson Crusoe by the Chilean government, which hoped to cash in on the appeal such a name might have for tourists looking for the ultimate island escape. Más Afuera, "farther out," which Selkirk never visited, was officially renamed Alexander Selkirk Island. A third island, nothing more than an islet off one end of Robinson Crusoe Island, was variously known as Goat Island or Santa Clara, which are alternative forms of "too insignificant for even government bureaucrats to bother with."

Around the time of the name changes, the Chileans built an airstrip on Isla Robinson Crusoe. As I abruptly discovered when we came swooping down onto it, the strip was a monument to audacity. It was located on the tail end of the island's dry side, in one of the few reasonably flat places, whose length was not much farther than the average Más a Tierra schoolboy could boot a soccer ball.

In later years, the airstrip would be paved. But when I visited, it was nothing more than an uncomfortably short stretch of red, volcanic soil from which somebody had leveled most, but not all, of the bumps and depressions. At both ends, the land plummeted far down into a blue and foamy sea.

However, we touched down with fewer jolts than I'd experienced during some 747 landings and taxied to a wooden, weather-beaten, three-room terminal. As soon as the propellers stopped spinning, we were greeted by a flock of chickens that contentedly pecked away beneath the plane while the pilot pecked away beneath the hood of a rust-stained jeep that was the official airport transport.

After the pilot was happy with his tinkering, we rode in the jeep down a switchback dirt road to a beautiful blue-water cove that was the remnant of a breached volcanic crater. Waiting for us in the cove were a couple of rough-shaven islanders in a double-ended outboard-powered open boat that looked as if Selkirk himself might have put into service.

We all piled into the boat, which was soon rising and plunging just seaward of pounding cannons of surf. After about an hour, we came to a green, hanging valley with another, more imposing valley beyond. One that I have since claimed struck me as looking as if it belonged in the very Highlands of Selkirk's Scotland. "English Bay," the pilot said to me. "Valley of the cave of Selkirk."

A short distance beyond English Bay, on Cumberland Bay, lay the village of San Juan Bautista, where virtually all 600 of the archipelago's residents lived. Most made their living by fishing for lobster. Patrons who paid up to fifty dollars each for the lobster in Santiago's better restaurants claimed they were the best tasting in the world. Those residents lived a life of isolation broken only by the occasional supply boat from Valparaíso and few small tourist planes from Santiago.

At San Juan Bautista, we were greeted on the town dock by two policemen, six or seven small boys, a dozen dogs, and the smell of pine trees.

One of the policemen, who, like his companion, wore a well-starched military-green uniform, asked me, "You have papers?"

I thought he wanted to see my passport, until he pointed to the daily newspaper from Santiago that I had stuffed into a side compartment of my duffel bag. I presented it to him, and our entourage continued up the dock as he read aloud the latest soccer scores.

The pilot, discovering that I had not arranged for a place to stay, volunteered to show me to Hosteria Green, one of only three small hotels on the island. It was on the other side of the village square—where a huge metal gong and a hammer on a rope served as the local version of 911—and across an unpaved thoroughfare covered with thick grass that I would later discover made it a nearly perfect soccer field.

Hosteria Green was a square, wood-framed building of four guest rooms with private baths. When we arrived, proprietor Reinaldo Green was standing out front, chatting with one of his neighbors about lobster. He spoke even less English than I did Spanish. But from his blue Los Angeles Dodgers baseball cap, I suspected we would get along just fine.

"He says he will be pleased to rent you a room," the pilot told me. "He says you are the only tourist on the island. He says he does not accept credit cards."

* * *

I spent days of mostly solitary exploration on Robinson Crusoe Island. Following a hiker's paradise of trails, I climbed to a place called Selkirk's Lookout, where there was a bronze tablet erected in his memory in 1869 by British sailors who got the date of his death wrong. Beneath a ruined fort near the village of tiny wooden houses, I crawled around in man-made caves that had served as cells in the days when the island was a penal colony. I walked up among pines and eucalypti and then down grassy hillsides into hidden valleys where streams flowed from the clouds.

In such an enchanted, lonely setting, it was easy to imagine, in the words of eighteenth-century poet William Cowper, from his work aptly titled "Verses Supposed to be Written by Alexander Selkirk," that I could be "... monarch of all I survey." It was easy to imagine, too, the effect such a setting could have had on Selkirk.

One of the more miscreant members of a large and continually squabbling family, the native of Fife, Scotland, had been brought before hometown authorities on several occasions, including once for "undecent behavior in the church." At age twenty-five, his response was to go to sea aboard what proved to be a pirate ship, one, as it happened, with a less than exemplary record of management-employee relations.

By the time the ship, the *Cinque Ports*, reached uninhabited Más a Tierra, which it visited to make repairs, replenish its water supply, and take on fresh meat by capturing some of the wild goats that roamed the island, Selkirk was at serious odds with the captain. He announced he was taking all his belongings ashore to stay, and he encouraged the rest of the crew to follow. None did.

Having had considerable experience in recognizing troublemakers, the captain was happy to let him go. So much so that when Selkirk, standing alone in the surf, began having second thoughts and begged to be taken back on board, pointing out that he had changed his mind, the captain's response, as he sailed away, was some taunting words and a wave goodbye.

Finding himself marooned alone on a desert island, Selkirk was initially so despondent that he considered taking his life. But slowly, he awoke to the possibilities of a world all his own. He became inventive at supplying his needs, laming small goats so that he could easily capture them for food when they grew up. And he worked diligently at improving his mind, making a close study of the few books he had with him, especially the Bible.

He was a far better Christian on the island, he would later say, than he had ever been before and would ever be again. When his clothes wore out, he took to wearing outfits fashioned from goatskins, although when he was finally rescued, the captain of the British ship that found him said he looked wilder than the skins' first owners.

As I roamed that same landscape where Selkirk had chased his goats and found his religion, I wondered if such a setting, in such circumstances, could have the same effect on us all.

Could I, for instance, become moved to act more responsibly about keeping people updated as to my travel plans?

It is the kind of question many people have asked. An essay about Selkirk's experience, written by Richard Steele in 1713, so fascinated journalist Daniel Defoe that much of the evidence indicates it served as a model for the novel (often considered the English language's first) that gave the world Robinson Crusoe.

The Life and Strange Surprizing Adventures of Robinson Crusoe of York, Mariner, was a best seller when first published in 1719 and has gone through countless editions and translations, including one in an Inuit language, accompanied by an illustration showing the hero standing near a palm tree and dressed in furs.

How the experience molded Selkirk's character might be judged by knowing that after he returned home, even though the booty he earned while pirating aboard the ship that rescued him made him relatively wealthy, he occasionally lived in a cave he dug in his parents' garden and tried to teach the local cats to dance.

* * *

As for me, when not exploring the landscape or contemplating what my response would be to finding myself entirely alone in it, another favorite way to pass the time was to sit in front of a little café by the dock and idle away the hours in conversation.

I talked about weather with a government meteorologist who confirmed that if the fast-approaching rainy season arrived before my plane, I might be on the island for months. I talked about politics with a man who saw everything in terms of lobster. And I talked about life in the United States with a young lady whose few words of English included the frequently repeated, "I no married."

But mostly, I talked to the captain of the monthly supply ship from Valparaíso and to the Chilean film crew, who, it turned out, had timed their visit to the island to coincide with that of the ship. The film crew was tracking a rumor that a particular species of sandalwood, once of vital economic importance to much of the South Pacific but thought to have been long extinct in the Juan Fernández Archipelago, might still survive in some of the isolated valleys of uninhabited Alexander Selkirk Island, the island "farther out."

The supply ship, departing in a few days under charter to the film crew, would be transporting them to the island. And, if a plane could not pick them up, it would be their ride back to the Chilean mainland.

Listening to their plans, I lost much of my interest in Robinson Crusoe Island, a place that suddenly seemed far too limited in its allure. Instead, I began plotting to see if I could wrangle an invitation to be on board when they sailed for Alexander Selkirk Island.

With the captain, who spoke excellent English, I bonded because of our mutual interest in everything nautical. That was a funny story about cooking for the crew of women, he told me. And another funny one, he said, would be when the film crew sat down to their first meal aboard his vessel, which, despite her many fine qualities, rolled her decks under in even the slightest sea. He would be happy to take me to Más Afuera, he said, after confirming that I could hold down the lunch he invited me aboard for, if it was OK with the film crew, at whose pleasure he would be serving.

With the film crew, I naturally discovered that despite our limited ability to communicate, we also had much in common, belonging as we did to the fraternity of journalists at large in the world. Yes, we agreed, editors typically had a wide-ranging number of faults. And yes, expense reimbursements always came late, and usually only after much complaining to somebody's assistant who seemed to think their time was so much more valuable than ours.

And yes, they decided, after we'd had a couple dozen or so pisco sours, the brandy-based national drink of Chile, they would be happy, as long as my story did not appear before theirs did, to have me share their adventure. They'd just slip the extra cost into their expense reports.

The only problem was that they planned to be on Selkirk for several weeks, and when they returned to Robinson Crusoe Island, there might not be room for me on the flight to Santiago. So, I might have to return on the long, sometimes rough passage to Valparaíso aboard the ship, which at that time of year had an uncertain schedule at best.

At a minimum, it would be a month before I returned to Santiago, and it could be much longer. And as there was no way for me to get in touch with my wife from the island, it would be at least that long before she might hear from me.

I gave it a lot of thought. I really wanted to go. I desperately wanted to go. And, technically, I was already missing anyway. But there is only so far a casualness about return dates can take you before it becomes too far.

So, in the end, I waved goodbye to my new friends as they sailed away for Alexander Selkirk Island, some of them waving back with noticeably diminishing enthusiasm as their otherwise fine little vessel began to roll.

7
The Lost Razor Blades of Zanzibar

Soon after Michael Shnayerson told me that *Condé Nast Traveler* wanted the Robinson Crusoe story, I pitched another idea to him. It was for a short, back-of-the-magazine piece about some medical machine a hotel in the Bahamas was installing, making it easier to stay there for well-off tourists who had kidney disease, I think. Which included nobody I knew.

I'd recently been to Nassau, and someone there told me about the machine, and I figured a brief story might be worth a few dollars. But in turning me down, Michael asked, "Do you want to be thought of as the writer who does stories about hotel medical devices or exotic islands?"

I opted for exotic islands and not only ended up writing about them often for *Traveler* but soon afterward discovered *Islands* magazine, where, over the next decade or so, I would have more stories published than I did anywhere else.

Today, *Islands* is entirely online and has nowhere the presence it once did. In its heyday, though, during the 1990s, it was among travel's best publications. And like *Condé Nast Traveler*, *Islands* seemed happy with letting a writer have their own voice. But unlike *Traveler*, *Islands* was only marginally interested in sharing "insider" information about where to sleep, eat, and shop. Instead, they mostly wanted to know about the one thing that should matter to travel writers above all else: In what ways are people in one place different from people in another, and in what ways are people everywhere the same?

So, they'd send me off to an island, often for weeks, because digging deep into places takes time, as any travel writer will insist. And I'd hang around wherever the locals congregated—a little restaurant or bar, maybe, especially if I were buying—and the stories would just come to me.

I'd start a conversation by asking about anything—the price of fish, the potency of the local drink, what the old times were like. I'd bring out my miniature tape recorder, set it unobtrusively on a table or countertop, and ask apologetically, "Do you mind?" And almost no one did because unless they are celebrities or politicians or anyone else accustomed to public life, people are nearly always flattered that someone is interested in their story. And for nothing more than a sympathetic ear, they are almost always willing to tell it.

Hours later, after hearing about everything from why the flowers seemed to be blooming earlier every year to who they thought a neighbor girl's new baby looked like, the conversation might end with, "You should talk to . . ."

And I would think: This is travel writing.

* * *

Islands' editor in chief, the person who gave me the time to let those stories happen, was Joan Tapper. She had come to the magazine in 1988 after serving for five years as the founding editor of *National Geographic Traveler*. She left *Islands* in 2001, but because of a line she used in some public forum, the Society of American Travel Writers newsletter, I think—"a writer of Bob Payne's caliber"—I continue to proclaim her brilliance.

The first story I did for Joan, which I didn't pitch until after I'd returned from the journey, was about the Indian Ocean island of Zanzibar.

A women's fashion magazine had assigned me to do a story about a walking safari in Zambia. And the way I often tried to work things was to get to some far place at somebody else's expense and then continue affordable distances from there on my own. So that is what I did, traveling from Zambia to Kenya, where I went on a game safari and visited Mount Kilimanjaro, then continued to Zanzibar, where the first thing I did was lose my luggage.

* * *

Some people claim I bring up the subject of lost luggage far more often than necessary, just so I can mention that the only time I've lost mine was on the way to Zanzibar. But they are mistaken. I bring up the lost luggage because it so well illustrates that for travel writers, the best trips are often those that go the most wrong.

My bag was lined up with all the others on the tarmac alongside a small prop plane in Nairobi. We were supposed to identify our pieces, and then they would be immediately loaded. I identified mine, and I thought it was immediately loaded. But when we arrived in Zanzibar, it was gone, forever. And the result was a story I could not otherwise have written.

The story began in afternoon heat, along narrow, shadowy streets where I told myself what I smelled was just a mixture of unfamiliar spices. I was trying to replace the contents of the lost bag in shops that were all the same: dark, tiny holes in the walls of stucco covered buildings that could most kindly be described as not having weathered well.

The shop fronts consisted of heavy wooden double doors, some with intricately carved doorposts and lintels, some inlaid with cup-size brass studs that would discourage the press of an angry crowd. Plastered to one door was a poster warning against the dangers of AIDS. On another was a placard advertising a swashbuckling pirates-versus-the-British film, the pirates seeming to be the good guys.

Considering that the only bargain I'd seen was a 100-pound sack of cloves, my shopping was not going too badly. I'd found a pair of khaki shorts almost my size and a souvenir T-shirt that said, "Don't worry, be happy" in Swahili.

I'd also been able to find—each item in a different shop—shampoo from England, shaving cream from Kenya, toothpaste from Germany, and a toothbrush "Manufactured under the surveillance of China National Light." The shaving cream came wrapped in an English-language newspaper, three weeks old, from which I learned that a man in Torquay, England, had been arrested and fined eighty pounds sterling for using threatening behavior toward an inflatable rubber doll.

What I hadn't been able to find was a razor. And I didn't think I would find one in the shop I had just entered. The shopkeeper and I had gone through the ritual greeting: "Jambo." (Hello.) "Habari?" (What news?) "Mzuri." (The news is good.) I'd scanned the meager stock in his glass case and on his dusty shelves. I'd repeated "razor" in English at several decibel levels. And, with little hope of success, I was going through the motions of shaving.

But praise Allah! As I brought my thumb across my throat in what I guess could have been mistaken for a slicing motion, the shopkeeper broke into a grin and rattled off something in Swahili that must have meant, "I know exactly what you want." He ushered me out of the shop, slammed shut the wooden doors, grabbed me by the hand, and set off through the crooked streets at such a pace that I was trailing sweat.

We went past black-garbed women who turned to stare, past grease-stained men squatting in the dirt repairing bicycles, past men hunched over ancient, clicking sewing machines, past a shop selling the skins of small brown animals, past Budda Auto Parts, to a . . . barbershop.

A lathered man was leaning back in a barber's chair. Four or five other men seemed to be waiting their turn. To the disappointment of my escort, I made it clear that I didn't want a shave, especially since one or two of the nicks in the barber's long-bladed razor looked as if they could have been the result of a sword fight.

Then began a rapid-fire, barbershop quintet discussion—accompanied by much flailing of arms and eventually involving anyone who happened to be passing in the street—about what exactly it was I did want. Finally, a consensus emerged, and I was whisked away again to yet another shop and another shopkeeper.

"Razor?" I asked him.

"Gillette?" he responded.

* * *

From my razor-shopping expedition, I concluded that Zanzibar—which, like Kathmandu and Timbuktu, is among the world's genuinely exotic-sounding places—knew very well how to cope with visitors from far-off lands.

A good thing, too, agreed almost everyone on the island with whom I spoke. Because, they said, it was about to be invaded. By the kind of invaders who arrived in groups aboard wide-body jets for stays of six or seven nights, tips and transfers included.

When Zanzibar joined mainland Tanganyika in 1964 to become the United Republic of Tanzania, its rulers drew what outside observers called a Spice Curtain of isolation around the island. But more recently, it had come to accept that tourism—long lumped together with the evils of colonialism, imperialism, and capitalism—was a necessary evil.

Following my visit, much of the tourist invasion came

to pass. Temporarily, it had been upended by COVID. But when that went away, there was little doubt that there would once again be direct charter flights from Europe and elsewhere, flourishing mass-market resorts, and upscale inns with rates topping $1,000 per night.

However, when I was there, Zanzibar was still a place where just about the only arrivals were adventure travelers and the occasional Coca-Cola distributor.

You could find the adventurers here and there on the miles of white-sand beaches so little visited that it didn't pay for muggers to stake them out. Or they'd be wandering in the lush green interior, breathing deeply beneath the short, compact trees that supplied the world with a significant portion of its cloves. And you could find them, usually lost and always claiming not to be, in the mazelike streets and passages of Stone Town, the oldest area of Zanzibar Town, the crowded, dusty city where the majority of the island's people lived.

Most stayed in hotels and guest houses that charged from eight to twelve dollars a night, including electricity and water, on the days when there were electricity and water. And most ate at food stalls in the Jamituri Gardens, where the local dishes, assuming you had already built an immunity to the intestinal disorders that remain a feature of African travel, were delicious and inexpensive.

A few, however, favored dining on locally caught lobster or prawns at the government-owned Bwawani Hotel, built by the Chinese, in the concrete block style, I believe, of their military hospitals, and charging the scandalously high room rate of forty-nine dollars a night for a single, which was easily the most expensive accommodation on the island.

Some of those adventurers spent their days peeking through the windows of the house where David Livingstone of "Dr. Livingstone, I presume?" once stayed. Or in the huge, musty Anglican cathedral, staring thoughtfully at the altar built on the spot where the whipping post stood when Zanzibar was the largest slave market on Africa's east coast. Or they might have their picture taken at the ruins of Maruhubi Palace, beside the pool where a sultan used to select the catch of the day from among his ninety-nine wives. The more nature-minded visited the natural history section of the National Museum, looking in vain—among the birds of Zanzibar, the butterflies of Zanzibar, and the bats of Zanzibar—for the cats of Zanzibar, made famous by Henry David Thoreau's I believe misguided pronouncement: "It is not worth the while to go round the world to count the cats in Zanzibar."

Late in the afternoon, when the heat began to lose some of its intensity, you could join these wanderers in chairs pulled up to the rail on the second-story veranda of the Africa House Hotel, which in an earlier time had been the British Club. While they sipped reasonably cold Tusker beers or Coca-Colas and discussed such vital issues as where to stay inexpensively in Nairobi, you could see them looking to the west. Beyond the soccer game on the grass at the edge of the seawall, beyond the backlit dhows ghosting across the water, beyond the faint black outline of the coast of mainland Tanzania, their eyes would be drawn to where the sun edged toward the orange-topped clouds that would determine whether the day was to end with yet another perfect sunset.

"I've heard there have already been people here looking to buy holiday cottages," said a bandanna-wearing Brit who claimed to be working his way around Africa as a professional golf caddy.

"The next thing you know, you'll be able to buy souvenir T-shirts everywhere," said Celeste, a Californian who had come to Zanzibar because, like me, she considered its name alone reason enough to make the trip.

And Diane, an Australian who I never saw in anything but

a tie-dyed dress that looked as if she had been wearing it since the decade of Flower Power, voiced the one word guaranteed to cast despair into the heart of almost any traveler contemplating a Third World paradise lost: "McDonald's."

To find anyone who thought opening Zanzibar to more tourists was a good idea, I had to go to the Zanzibaris themselves. And I had to go no farther than the four or five taxi drivers who spent most of every day parked in the shade of the casuarina trees at the entrance to the Bwawani Hotel.

"More tourists, more spice tours," said one driver.

Another, Ahmed, who described himself as a Zanzibari first and a Tanzanian second (a relatively common view the mainland government would undoubtedly not have been pleased to hear), said that Zanzibar, unlike mainland Tanzania, had been wealthy before unification. With help from the outside, it could become so again. "Tourism could bring us help," he said.

"But what if it brings people who want to make Zanzibar more like the places they come from?"

"We are Zanzibaris," he said. "Like a flag, we shift with the wind."

* * *

Ahmed obviously knew something of Zanzibar's past. The wind—the monsoon blowing steadily in one direction for half the year, then reversing itself and blowing just as steadily for the other half—had played a significant role in shaping Zanzibar's climate and history. It brought the two rainy seasons that made Zanzibar look like the Garden of Eden. And for centuries, it brought the slaving dhows that made Zanzibar a hell on earth.

By the mid-1800s, Zanzibar's slave market exported some 20,000 slaves a year, primarily to Arab countries. Its ruler,

Seyyid Said, the sultan of Oman and Zanzibar, was so powerful that he controlled a million-square-mile area of Africa stretching to the great inland lakes. As the saying went—in Zanzibar—"When the flute plays in Zanzibar, they dance on the lakes."

Seyyid Said made Zanzibar a force to be reckoned with. But he did not reckon with the force of the West, especially Britain, who would eventually turn the sultans of Zanzibar into puppet rulers who would dance to the tune of European colonialism until the early 1960s.

In 1964, when Zanzibar became part of Tanzania, the young nation hoped to become a model for self-reliant socialism in Africa. But by all accounts, the model, based on collective farming techniques, never came together.

"An economic basket case" is how one observer described Tanzania in an article in *Time* magazine. The problem was compounded by a decline in world demand for cloves, a major source of Zanzibar's foreign exchange earnings.

When I arrived, the government seemed to be looking for the parts, and the glue, to build a new economic model based on tourism.

And tourism was already affecting Zanzibar. I had that demonstrated to me one day when four of us banded together to hire a van to ride across the southern end of the island to the beach at Bwejuu.

In the morning, in a dusty marketplace where a thousand Zanzibaris seemed to have some business connected with the loading and unloading of a half-dozen buses, we met at a pre-arranged spot. The van was already waiting, and waiting with it were the young driver, who was wearing a Bob Marley T-shirt, and Ali, the driver's interpreter, who spoke English about as well as you would expect from someone who had learned it in a schoolroom in a country that had been isolated from the West for more than two decades.

After reconfirming the price, which was not too much more than the price the driver had agreed upon the previous evening, our party climbed aboard, and the van pulled out onto busy Creek Road. However, before we were even entirely on the road, it stalled. And, despite the driver's grinding the ignition for several minutes, it refused to start again. I remarked that we might be out of gas—a suggestion, I gathered from the driver's mutterings, that was not particularly well-received.

"Plenty gas," said Ali.

The driver got out, made one slow perambulation of the van, got back in, ground the ignition a few more times, and muttered again.

"What did he say?" asked Nigel, a tall, slender Christian missionary worker based in Mombasa, a Kenyan coastal resort he described as similar to Zanzibar, with the rough edges already smoothed off.

"He says you pay now, we buy gas," said Ali.

"No. If it doesn't start, we don't pay anything," said Donna, a Chicagoan who had something to do with banking. Nigel, who had been in Africa longer than any of us, counseled patience.

The driver and Ali talked for a few minutes. Glumly, it seemed to me. Then, the driver, slapping himself on the forehead, appeared to be struck by a wonderful solution. He pulled out a crumpled wad of Tanzanian shillings and waved them in the direction of a place in the market that Ali said sold gas.

"In Africa," Nigel said quietly, "the answer is almost always patience."

Ali happily got out and pushed us in the direction of the gasoline seller. We all happily got out and pushed. A group of boys in the street, engaged in one of the seventy or eighty soccer games taking place on Zanzibar at any given moment, happily abandoned their game long enough to push. And soon, we were driving out of town on what the four of us were repeatedly assured, to the point of making us have our doubts, was a full tank of gas.

With reggae music blasting from the driver's tape player and red dust pouring in like surf through windows that wouldn't roll up, we flew south at a suicidal twenty-five miles per hour on the cratered tarmac surface of a road that could not have had a nickel spent on its maintenance since the day the British left. The driver and Ali shouted greetings to people all along the way.

Slowing down only when a particularly jarring bump would make it necessary for Nigel to reach under the dashboard and reconnect the wires to the tape player, we eventually reached the beach at Bwejuu, which we found as lovely as we had been told it would be: Sixteen uninterrupted miles of white sand, shallows for wading in, sun for baking under, and enough coconut palms for everyone to nap in the shade of their own.

I was looking for my own when I spotted a small boy sitting beside a pile of palm fronds that he was weaving into what I assumed was roofing material. He made such a perfect portrait of innocence and industry that I got out my camera.

I'd already learned that outside of Stone Town, many people on Zanzibar would run away or become angry at the sight of a camera. But he grinned, so I took my picture. When I finished, he said something to me that I asked Ali to translate.

"He wants you to show him the picture," Ali said.

I was amused but embarrassed, too. The boy had apparently taken it for granted that I possessed magic powers, and, as painful as it was, in those days before digital cameras, I was going to have to admit otherwise.

While I explained the mysteries of photography, including that it would take me some time to get his picture developed, Ali translated. The boy studied me for a moment and then spoke again.

"He says," Ali told me, "You might want to get a Polaroid."

*   *   *

Sometimes, I think about that boy and a world from which Polaroid cameras, and film of any kind, have all but vanished. And I wonder if, in the digital age, any mysteries will remain forever. Then, I ask myself how a man could survive ninety-nine wives. Or make his way around Africa as a professional golf caddy. Or be unhappy that he lost his luggage on Zanzibar.

8
Life, Death, and Rejection on the Amazon

The first time it occurred to me that travel writing can kill you, I was rafting a whitewater river in Costa Rica for a story that would end up in one of the columns I did for *iExplore.com*.

Some whitewater rivers are unquestionably killers, and all but the very skillful or very foolish river-runners stay away from them. But even rivers routinely run by commercial outfitters can put you at some risk.

Too late to do anything about it, you learn that the local name for the rapids ahead of you means "Where the Good Die Young." Then, down you rush, sweeping to one side of a bone-crushing-size boulder and slamming into a wall of tumbling white foam that inundates the raft with what feels like the force of someone trying to clean out your nostrils with a fire hose.

"Forward hard," says your guide. What he means is "Paddle for your lives."

You are paddling for your life. But because your life seems to be taking a different direction than that of some of your companions, the raft doesn't get as far to the left or right as the guide knows is necessary. An enormous wave that looks like a haystack from hell rears up in front of you. The back of the raft dips under. The river is pouring in.

Amidst a roar of water so deafening that you can't tell if

you are the one shouting, the raft stands nearly on its tail. It twists one way, then another, but somehow, miraculously, lands right side up, and you find yourself downstream of the wave.

People are in the water. Behind you, a woman who you recollect as having the bearing of the matriarch of an old-money New England dynasty is struggling to pull herself back aboard. You reach down, grab her by the top of her life jacket, and dump her into the bottom of the raft as if she were a sack of—old money. You reach out again and snag a paddle and a tube of sunscreen that have been holding their own in the race downstream.

Everybody is aboard, and the only injury seems to be to a dentist from New Jersey who, at this moment, wouldn't trade the modest amount of blood trailing down from a scrape on his knee for a hundred thousand frequent flyer miles. You are exhausted. You are exhilarated.

Knowing that the river grows less violent from here on down, you raise a paddle-clenched fist and join the chorus of affirmative responses to the old-money matriarch's shout of "Yee-hah. Bring on the big water."

* * *

Our Costa Rican river, though, wasn't like that, having only a few rapids that needed paying attention to. Still, some in our group were first-time paddlers, and some were nervous, and one of them asked the river guide if anyone had been hurt on previous trips.

"Only on the bus ride," the guide answered reassuringly.

I thought he was joking, until we got on the bus—which appeared to be under the protection of a likeness of Jesus mounted above the driver's head—and bounced our way toward the put-in spot on an extremely narrow, unpaved mountain road whose outer edge seemed to drop off into Deep Space.

As are the citizens of virtually every Latin American country, Costa Ricans are mad about soccer. And on the day we rode the bus, the Ticos, as they often call themselves, were playing a game that, if they won, would do something like advance them further in World Cup competition than Costa Rica had ever been before.

Our driver was listening to the game on a radio, turned up loud enough so that we mostly uncomprehending Americans would not miss a play. Which was fine until one lightning moment, when the Costa Rican team made its move, the bus drifted to the very precipice, and our driver raised both hands towards Jesus and shouted, "Score!"

That's when I thought we all might die, but if we lived what a great story it would make.

* * *

The death writers fear most, though, is one in which a story is killed. And one of the first stories I would write for *Outside* magazine got killed. It happens to everyone, I know, for all sorts of reasons. And I would write other stories for *Outside*. And see this one published on *i.Explore.com*. But as a writer, it is your instinct to feel all the guilt and wonder if the magazine will ever again trust you enough to pay expenses in advance.

I was especially sorry, though, to see *Outside* kill that particular story. Because when I tell people how I waded out of a South American river as a contingent of Venezuelan soldiers scrambled down an embankment toward me, clicking rounds into the chambers of their rifles as they came, it would be nice if I could show published corroboration.

Maybe the story didn't work because I wasn't listening closely enough when the editors told me what they wanted. Either that or the idea of *Outside* readers attempting to follow in my footsteps frightened the magazine's legal department.

I wanted to do a piece about a jungle survival school, where they would teach you how to live off the land and then abandon you in a suitably hostile environment, to see how you did. And somebody gave me the name of Jerzy Majcherczyk. Polish-born but living in the U.S., Majcherczyk, who went by the more easily pronounceable name of Yurek, was an organizer of extreme adventure tours. He said he had no survival schools to recommend at the moment but was about to undertake an expedition to South America that might require those skills.

With a fellow adventurer and fellow Pole, a photographer named Zbigniew Bzdak, who friends often called Zbig, Yurek was going to attempt a river journey to a remote area of Venezuela that was home to the Yanomami. The Yanomami were a group of Indians who were called, apparently not without reason, "The Fierce People."

If the journey proved successful, said Yurek, he hoped to offer it as a commercial adventure tour.

"Please come," he said. "If you survive, this will be good."

They were interesting individuals, Yurek and Zbig. As students with pro-democracy leanings in communist Poland in 1979, they'd left the country (fled might be a more accurate word) as part of a kayaking team known as Canoandes. Over the next few years, they would run some of South America's wildest whitewater rivers, including the mightily feared Colca, which they were the first to descend, alive.

I'd heard, too, that on one expedition—which Yurek hadn't been along for—Zbig, on a lonely stretch of river, was captured and had a rifle put to his head by members of the violent Peruvian insurgent group, Sendero Luminoso, or The Shining Path.

Both men had moved to the U.S. and become American citizens. But South America still had a hold over them, and the expedition, although it didn't involve whitewater, would be a chance for them to experience more of it.

My wife was not happy about me traveling with them.

"It'll be all right," I tried to reassure her. "These guys are old hands at this kind of thing. And from what I can tell, they know how to get out of trouble."

But she wasn't reassured. "People who know how to get out of trouble," she said, "are usually people who have a habit of getting into it."

That is why I thought it best not to mention that a recent book I had greatly enjoyed, *In Trouble Again,* by Redmond O'Hanlon, tells a story that takes place in the same area Yurek and Zbig were heading.

O'Hanlon had made contact with the famously violent Yanomami and taken part with them in an infamous ritual. The ritual involved ingesting, by way of having it forced up his nostrils by a man on the other end of a very long blowpipe, a powerful hallucinatory drug called yopo. Among yopo's potentially harmful side effects was making the women of the fiercest men on earth start to look good.

* * *

On a Sunday in March, Yurek, Zbig, and I met in Manaus, Brazil, were the Rio Negro flows into the Amazon, and waitresses and long-distance truck drivers were in the streets, dancing the lambada, as they apparently did every Sunday.

Yurek was blond, sinewy, and all business. He was also a devout Catholic, which would prove to be surprisingly useful. Zbig was easy going and easily likable. Of more vital interest, though, he had stovepipe legs that made him the person you wanted at the other end of a rope if it were the only thing keeping you from being swept down a deadly whitewater river.

From Manaus, we planned to fly some 600 miles up the Rio Negro to the Brazilian river town of Sao Gabriel of the

Rapids. Then, we'd travel upstream by outboard-powered canoe for four or five days to where the borders of Brazil, Columbia, and Venezuela came together. There, we would turn onto a smaller stream, the Casiquiare, which had the distinction of connecting South America's two greatest river systems, the Amazon and the Orinoco, and flowing through the heart of Yanomami territory.

However, a potential problem was that everyone we talked with in Manaus told us we would never make it to the Casiquiare. Officials all along the route would turn us back, everyone said, assuring us that even if we did reach the river, we would not be allowed to travel on it.

The Venezuelan government, mostly for reasons that involved illegal gold mining, wanted to keep people away. And the Yanomami, who still hunted their foes with poison-tipped arrows and dressed in a nearly naked fashion now seldom seen except on the beaches of Rio de Janeiro, did not exactly greet outsiders with coffee and doughnuts at trailside welcome stations.

It all seemed academic to me, anyway, because at the Manaus airport, the operations manager made a special trip out of his office to tell us there would be no seats for us to Sao Gabriel. The eighteen-passenger plane was overbooked and overweight, he said.

Seemingly unconcerned by the news, Zbig chatted up the gate agent while Yurek, the cross he always wore around his neck flashing in the sunlight, made friends with the baggage handlers, the people who were mopping the terminal floor, and anyone else who walked by. To several of them, I believe Yurek showed a photo of Pope John Paul II.

When the plane left, we were on it, a trio of drug traffickers having been bumped to make room for us. Too bad for them, I thought, that the ticket agent was a devout Catholic. For most of the flight, though, which was over vast areas of rainforest broken only occasionally by scattered clearings along oxbow rivers, I did wonder how the gold miner two rows up from us might react when he discovered we were the reason the wooden crates of mining equipment he'd checked in with were left behind.

We landed and got away from the airport, quickly, without incident and were soon relaxing in a Sao Gabriel restaurant that sat on a bluff overlooking the most imposing rapids on the Rio Negro. Fortunately, the rapids were on the downstream side of where we would board the thirty-five-foot outboard-powered canoe we had rented for our upriver journey.

"Ah, senhors, perfecto," said Zbig, using most of the Portuguese he knew, as the sun began to touch the outline of trees across the river

"Yes," said Yurek, "All except for the name, Sao Gabriel of the Rapids. This is too long for tourists to remember. In my brochures, perhaps I think I will call it Rapid City."

Later in the evening, after a few caipirinhas, Brazil's national hard-liquor drink of distilled sugar cane and lime, I asked Zbig about the time The Shining Path attacked him.

He was on the Apurimac River, which is the source of the Amazon, with a group of rafters, seven, I think, including an American named Joe Kane, who would write about their adventure in his book, *Running the Amazon*. After being shot at from up on a canyon rim one morning, they were confronted on shore by a gang of men dressed chiefly in tatters. One of the men was armed with a rifle, another with a submachine gun.

The man with the rifle shouted angrily and put it to Zbig's head, while the others proclaimed that they were Sendero Luminoso. After some tense moments and then hours of negotiation, during which the rafters were most afraid that the gang would discover Kane was an American, they were relieved of some of their supplies and personal effects and let go.

"And the Senderos? What were they like?" I asked.

"Oh, not so bad, once you got to know them," Zbig said.

We departed Sao Gabriel early the next morning, the sky clouded only slightly by the parting words of the man who had rented us the canoe: "Do not expect to make it."

The man said that within his memory, maybe a hundred outsiders had started upriver to the junction of the Rio Negro and the Casiquiare. And none of them, he said, had been able to get permission from the Venezuelan military authorities in San Carlos de Rio Negro, a village near the junction, to travel the Casiquiare itself.

To which Yurek responded only by fingering his cross.

* * *

When the naturalist Alfred Russel Wallace came upstream from Sao Gabriel to the Casiquiare in 1848, he described his canoe as "thirty-five feet long and seven broad, with a semicircular roof, high enough to sit up comfortably within."

Which would work just as well for a description of ours. The only difference was that while Wallace's relied on muscle power, a forty-horsepower outboard motor pushed us along. An identical motor lay in the bottom of the canoe, and I was happy to observe, as we got deeper into the jungle, that our driver, Joaquim, slept with an arm around each of them.

Beyond Sao Gabriel, the black-water river was quiet-flowing, the vegetation along its banks broken only rarely by small Indian villages, several of which we visited. At one, we commended the villagers' wisdom in turning to modern medicine to combat the common run of minor ailments while continuing to depend on the rainforest plants for what they considered the important stuff, such as snakebite remedies and contraceptives. At another, Yurek suggested to the head man that the villagers begin thinking about something they could make to sell to tourists.

These villagers, to be clear, were not the feared Yanomami but seemingly far more civilized people. Which is to say, they wore civilized dress, the currently fashionable items appearing to be caps and T-shirts bearing the name of a Brazilian politician whose operatives must have spent many nights sleeping in hammocks.

And all seemed friendly. Friendly in the reserved way you might be if a group of Amazon Indians suddenly appeared in your living room and wanted to know if you had any crafts to sell that might interest other groups of Amazon Indians arriving at some vague time in the future.

We could communicate with them because, along with the driver, our canoe had come with the translator option. He was a young Brazilian ex-urbanite named Gilberto who claimed to speak Geral, a trade language the Indians used so that one tribe could talk with another. But I suspect he knew only the words for hello, goodbye, and snake.

"They are saying come back any time," he said as we pulled away from each village.

* * *

We spent our first night in a one-family riverside clearing that its residents called Icana, where we hung our hammocks from the beams of a guesthouse still under construction. We hung them there even though the family's patriarch, Valentine, who was three or four generations removed from an original mix of Spanish and Indian blood, wanted us to sleep in the family church.

The church had been built by Valentine's grandfather, who topped it with a wooden cross that—until Yurek jury-rigged it back into place—had been tilting at a crazy angle for probably a quarter of a century. Valentine said visitors had always hung their hammocks in the church, including the missionary priests who occasionally came to call.

But Yurek, devout Catholic that he was, was outraged. "Sleep in the church?" he asked. "Do you make a joke?"

Valentine wasn't joking. He said the church leaked less than any other available structure. And it's four solid walls would protect us from the many dangers of the jungle. Dangers such as the pit viper that had bitten one of the family pets—a limping, one-eyed, rooster-like bird whose only attractive quality seemed to be that it liked snakes even less than it liked people.

But Valentine's reasoning didn't sway Yurek, who hung his hammock in the unfinished guesthouse and insisted that Zbig and I do the same.

While Yurek was checking on the arrangements, Valentine, who spoke Portuguese and a little English, and, for reasons I thought best left unexplored, wanted to learn the English for "You are like a flower," said that during the night it would rain. And that because the unfinished guest house had a roof but no walls, we would get wet.

In the night, it rained, and we got wet. But in the morning, Yurek was able to leave with the satisfaction of knowing that he had not slept in the church. And Zbig and I were able to leave with the satisfaction of having heard the opinion, expressed by a resident of one of the most remote places in South America, that "You meet all kinds around here."

As we departed Icana, Valentine thanked us for the church's repairs and told us we were welcome back any time, which he said would probably be soon. As he, too, gave us little chance of getting on the Casiquiare.

Later that day, as we approached our first frontier checkpoint, I grew increasingly nervous about how we might be received at the Colombian border, as most of what I knew about Colombia had been learned from the television show *Miami Vice*.

"Oh, there is nothing to worry about," Zbig said. "Unless

you are a journalist. Or an American."

He stretched out in the canoe, pulled his hat over his face, and pretended to nap, which is when I took the opportunity to slip my reporter's notebook into one of the side pockets of his camera bag.

I need not have concerned myself, though. The border crossing took us only slightly more time than it did the supply-boat captain who arrived just before we did, carrying a gallon jug of wine. In fact, I think that the lone Colombian guard, preoccupied with seeing that he didn't burn his dinner, never opened our passports.

Just over the border was, to my surprise, a tourist lodge. Named El Kiosco, the lodge had six rooms, all without bath, unless you counted the river. It had cold beer. It had cold Coca-Cola. It had a pool table. And, as a result of the outside world's seemingly false assumption that you were as likely to run into the cartel crowd in one part of Colombia as in another, it had an occupancy rate that for years had hovered around zero.

The lodge was owned and run by a genial former professor, Matias Vasquez, who, because it appeared that the front desk could get along just fine in his absence, served as an impromptu guide for the next part of our journey up the river.

It was Matias who showed us how to attract the attention of the pink-bellied botos, or river dolphins, by slapping the surface of the river with a canoe paddle. It was Matias who pointed out orchids, birds, butterflies, and—most wonderful of all—the lack of mosquitos. Black-water rivers like the Rio Negro are so high in naturally produced tannins (which gives them and tea their dark color) that mosquito larvae can't survive in them, he said.

And it was Matias who made casual mention, as we hacked our way through an overgrown rubber plantation during a side excursion, of the big cats rumored to be in the vicinity. Over the years, the families who cultivated the small clearings at the river's edge reported that jungle cats had carried off a few pigs and one small cow, Matias said. "But the cats are like tourists. They don't come very often, and they don't stay very long."

A day beyond El Kiosco, we arrived at the little Colombian town of San Felipe, near where the Casiquiare flows into the Rio Negro. Usually, tourists wouldn't stay overnight in the town. But Matias' friend, the port captain, redistributed some of his children to provide a room for us in his official residence, a house so grand that it had screens on the windows and indoor plumbing, of sorts.

The captain, who I think was actually a sergeant, confirmed what we had heard all along. Outsiders needed permission to travel on the Casiquiare, and the Venezuelans never gave it.

He said he would see what he could do, but he wasn't optimistic. "Sadly," he said, "the Venezuelans are less compromising in these matters than my countrymen."

In the end, the captain decided what he could do was take us across the river in his patrol boat. But because he could not touch Venezuelan soil, we would have to jump from the boat's bow and wade ashore.

We immediately accepted his offer, although on the way over, because it was the responsible thing to do, I gave him a piece of paper with our names on it, in case someday somebody came looking for us. I decided, too, that I might as well afford myself every advantage. So, following Yurek's lead, just before jumping, I made the sign of the cross.

As we landed on the shore, near the edge of San Carlos de Rio Negro, a cry went up from above us, and armed Venezuelan soldiers swarmed down the bank. Things got uncomfortable for a while after that, until the soldiers went through our passports, two of which contained names so long that the letters almost ran off the edge of the page.

One of the soldiers, who from his gym shorts and Reeboks appeared to be high-ranking, slowly scrutinized us, scrutinized the passports again, and finally turned to a camouflage-garbed subordinate. "Go get Father Kaczmarczyk," he said.

Two hours later, after a reunion of countrymen, one of whom had spent seventeen years in the Amazon basin with only one trip back to Poland in all that time, we were on the Casiquiare.

* * *

Because the kind of connecting link it forms between two major river systems is so rare in nature, the Casiquiare's existence was still a subject of controversy when, in 1801, Alexander Von Humboldt, almost half a century before Alfred Russel Wallace's visit, set out to settle the question once and for all. The journey would become the foundation for his reputation as one of South America's greatest explorers—and worst prophets. Humboldt not only found the Casiquiare, he predicted it would one day become the door for an enormously wealthy trade route.

The explorer's efforts did have at least one trade-related effect, however. It convinced Yurek that he would call the commercial version of our journey, should it ever materialize, "In Humboldt's Track."

(Actually, Humboldt reached the Casiquiare by traveling up the Orinoco, not the Rio Negro. But, having written a little bit of advertising, I could appreciate that such a technicality was hardly a reason to let go of a catchy phrase.)

As evidence of how wrong Humboldt had been in his prophecy, fewer people lived in the area surrounding the Casiquiare when we arrived than when Humboldt had. And the nearly untouched jungle along its banks still sheltered many descendants of such animals as the jaguar that carried off his pet dog. In fact, about the only people in the area were the Yanomami and the gold miners who were, in some cases, trying to exterminate them.

There'd been much controversy about how fierce the Yanomami really are, their reputation based in no small part on the observations of an anthropologist, Napoleon Chagon, who spent years living with them before publishing, in 1968, *Yanomamo: The Fierce People*. Because of Chagon's claims, the book was so controversial that it was alleged to be the best-selling anthropology textbook of all time.

Other researchers had disputed the claims and continue to. But the Yanomami were unquestionably hard people, as they needed to be. As far back as the 1940s, contact with outsiders, including road builders, researchers, ranchers, and, especially, goldminers, had exposed them, sometimes intentionally, to diseases, such as measles and the flu, that proved to be devastating. And not long after we were there, five gold miners were convicted of genocide by a Brazilian court for murdering a group of Yanomami, including a baby.

*   *   *

For us, our brief time on the Casiquiare (even with Father Kaczmarczyk's endorsement, we could get only a day) proved to be something less than full contact. Except that the water's color changed from black to brown, the river, wider than I'd expected, looked much like the river we'd been traveling for the past few days. And I'm not sure if we ever actually saw any Yanomami, in part because we left San Carlos with an armed military escort.

At one clearing, where a few dwellings looked as if they had been recently abandoned—about five minutes before our arrival—we did see two young Indian boys, who the soldiers claimed were Yanomami.

But I had my doubts. Both boys were indeed armed with blowpipes that stood taller than they did. And they did solemnly hold their ground as we approached. But they were dressed much too fashionably, which is to say, in cast-off clothing perhaps collected by a church in Poland from its parishioners. And the Yanomami, I had been told, still wore nothing more than a loincloth.

I may have been wrong about the boys, though. Because as we were standing by the riverbank, one of them spotted a movement high up in the trees on the far side of the clearing. And almost before I realized what was happening, he'd put a dart in flight toward a perched bird I could hardly make out.

The boy missed the bird, but only by a fraction of an inch, striking the branch just below its feet, and sending it off, a white blur, into the jungle.

"Hoo, hoo," chuckled his companion.

We gestured, though, that we were very impressed with the boy's marksmanship. And they, encouraged by the soldiers, offered to trade for both weapons, darts included. I got mine for the compass I wore on a leather cord around my neck.

That's when the boys were flabbergasted to discover that there could be people in the world so primitive that they didn't know which end of a blowpipe is supposed to go in your mouth.

I thought they would die laughing. In fact, I hoped so.

9

Bora Bora Might Just be Home

The pain of having the Amazon story killed was greatly diminished by Joan Tapper at *Islands* asking me if I wanted to go to Bora Bora.

Of course, I did. It was an exotic island and somewhere I hadn't been. But there was a problem.

An editor I knew from another magazine had put me in touch with somebody who wanted help writing a book. The book, *Norm Abram's New House*, would follow the construction of the personal home of the master carpenter on the PBS series, *This Old House*.

I helped Norm put together an outline. And the figure they offered me to see the manuscript all the way through was ten times what going to Bora Bora would pay. But because of the scheduling, I could not do both.

Over the objections of several voices—reason among them—I chose Bora Bora, because I am a traveler, and an appreciator of exotic islands, not an observer of houses being built, however nice the houses, and the compensation, might be.

And soon enough, I was sitting in one of Bora Bora's restaurants, trying to decide what to order for lunch and feeling guilty because I was thinking of having, yet again, the marinated fish salad known as poisson cru.

So, I consulted my waitress, a woman who knew something about love. Or so I gathered from the word "Love" tattooed in English on her forearm. I asked her what her favorite island dishes were.

"Me, I like the canned tuna, the canned Spam, and, most of all, the canned corn beef," she said.

I thought she might be kidding, because she accompanied her answer with giggles and then fled to the kitchen.

But after lunch, when I rode my rented bicycle into Bora Bora's biggest settlement, Vaitape, I stopped at Chin Lee's grocery and found a well-stocked supply of the very items the waitress had named. As I stood looking at the jumbled shelves, a local man politely shouldered his way in front of me to pick up three, four, and, finally, after some hesitation, five cans of corned beef.

Overcome by a curiosity that, not for the first time in my life, I would regret, I bought a can, took it back to my hotel room, and sat down to eat it. The contents, which I had identified, correctly, I hoped, by the smiling cow on the label, was so high in fat that its color was almost white. The smell, although not immediately identifiable to me, was what I have forever after thought of as long-dead bovine. And as for the taste, I got down one small bite. The rest could remain uneaten, as far as I was concerned, until the cows came home.

I was intrigued. With a lagoon that amounted to a seafood takeout and ripe coconuts on every palm tree (except those that had been removed so guests would not risk injury while on hotel property), could the locals really prefer canned meat?

"Yeah, they love the stuff," said Richard Postma, an expatriate American who had been on Bora Bora for so long that he spoke fluent Tahitian and wore a thigh-circling, self-administered tattoo of traditional Polynesian design that put to shame the American jailhouse style that in those days was all too frequently seen in Papeete.

I was questioning Richard as he allowed me to steer his

forty-six-foot sailing catamaran, *Vehia*, across a lagoon whose waters displayed more variations of the blues than an after-hours jam session at a Memphis nightclub. As the other guests stretched out on the netting between *Vehia's* two hulls, blissfully unaware of who was at the wheel, Richard told me that the taste for canned meat was a legacy of the American occupation of the island during World War II.

The war, he said, was a time remembered with much fondness by the older locals, who never saw any of the horrors of conflict, only the generosity of thousands of young American boys with PX privileges. As a result, Bora Bora remained a rare place where people genuinely liked Americans and canned meat products.

It was a fondness strengthened by the fact, said Richard, that the Americans had the good sense, in the eyes of the Bora Borans, to come in, share their wealth, make love to their women ("The locals think it's a great trait to be part American.") and then leave.

He said Bora Borans thought the American way made infinitely more sense than the approach taken by the French, who had been administering much of Polynesia since the 1800s and were increasingly criticized for introducing the region to atomic testing and—of greater concern to many—the work ethic.

Based on my imagining of Bora Bora, I found much that was as I had expected. There was the physical beauty. James A. Michener had seen to that: "To come back to Bora Bora at the close of day after a long trip in a small boat and to see the setting sun illuminate the volcanic tower, massive and brooding in gold, is to see the South Pacific at its unforgettable best."

And there were the happy, smiling people. Again Michener: "People...as attractive as their island, the most natural and uninhibited Polynesians of all..."

But it is often the unexpected discoveries that make a place special and form the basis of the stories you tell.

* * *

The first unexpected discovery many people make about Bora Bora is that it belongs to the same small group of French Polynesian islands that includes the perennial beauty-contest finalists Tahiti and Moorea. The group is called the Society Islands, so named by Captain James Cook because the 150-mile string of them—including the lesser-known beauties, Huahine, Raiatea, Tahaa, and Maupiti—seemed to him sociably close together.

Bora Bora, or Pora Pora, as it was originally spelled, is among the smallest of the Society Islands. Five miles across and nineteen in circumference, it is small enough that during its pre-European history, its warriors had to develop a unique talent to survive, a talent immortalized in a line from a Polynesian chant: "Pora Pora with the fleet that strikes both ways." This does not refer to Polynesia's liberal attitudes toward sexual preference but to the fact that Bora Borans introduced a concept into warfare that had never occurred to their neighbors: the sneak attack.

Centuries had passed since the last of Bora Bora's war canoes, their paddles muffled, arrived at a neighboring island for a surprise party. Now, Bora Bora was culturally so close to Tahiti that Bora Borans spoke Tahitian, better, they said, than the residents of Tahiti did, and referred to themselves generically as Tahitians. Yet, unexpectedly, modern warfare had played a significant role in shaping Bora Bora's culture—and setting it apart from even its nearest neighbors.

In 1942, Bora Bora was taken over by the U.S. military as the site for a refueling base. Some 4,500 American troops were sent there to build the base and defend it. Most of the service members, the majority of them men, arrived not knowing where they were or what they would find. According to one of them, naval officer James A. Michener, what they found was paradise.

It was such a paradise, Michener later wrote, that unlike other Pacific islands during the war, where the enlisted men became restless and wanted to go home if they were left too long, the enlisted men stationed on Bora Bora didn't want to go home at all and would "raise merry hell" when efforts were made to send them.

Among the attractions, there was the palm-fringed reef, which surrounded the expansive lagoon, which in turn surrounded the high, green island. There was the sun, the trade winds, and the golden white sand. And there was, also from Michener, this: "The word vahine (woman) surfaced in almost everything I learned about Bora Bora."

Another naval officer wrote that "The younger women were strikingly beautiful." And yet another, presumably not very popular with the troops, said, "When we first got there, the women just wore a sarong with bare breasts. We showed them how to wear tops."

* * *

Fifty years after the first U.S. service members arrived, I followed. And one of the first people I talked with was a seventy-two-year-old American named Hysler Hope Eastburn, who I met in the open-air lobby of the Hotel Bora Bora. Pappy Hope, as the locals called him, had first come to Bora Bora in February 1942 as a twenty-two-year-old U.S. Army private.

Now a retired professional gardener who had visited Bora Bora every year for the past eighteen, he walked with a slow, slightly bent gait that served as a reminder of just how long ago World War II had taken place. Yet not two minutes after I'd met him, he was insisting, despite my fear of being held responsible for his demise, that he show me the way up a steep, overgrown path leading to two of the eight 30,000-pound coastal defense guns the Americans had brought with them to the island.

The climb, near the Matira Restaurant, took us about twenty minutes. When we arrived at the top, we were both sweating, I, perhaps, the more profusely.

"Tough walk," I said, in what I hoped sounded like a condescending tone.

"You ought to try it dragging them guns."

The guns—huge, rusting things—had been dragged up the side of the hill, using ropes and, I presume, a full inventory of the kind of language for which army sergeants are known. It took 400 men, including Pappy Hope, five months to get the job done.

"I think of it as paradise now, but I didn't in them days," he said as we looked from the hilltop toward the pearl-white necklace of surf that encircles the lagoon.

"There was them guns to keep us busy. And the land crabs."

The land crabs, he said, had been the real enemy on Bora Bora, which the Japanese never attacked. "You'd hang your socks on the line, the wind would blow them down, and the land crabs would drag them into a hole. Two or three days later, the crabs would bring them out again, all chewed up."

By 1946, the U.S. service members were gone from Bora Bora. But even during my visit, the islanders, even the ones who weren't around during the war (which was most of them), still talked about Americans with the kind of enthusiasm kids usually reserve for a favorite aunt or uncle who comes loaded with gifts but never stays around long enough to become an authority figure.

"Americans built the airport that lets us have tourists," one local woman told me. "Without it, we'd still be working on coconuts."

The woman, generously girthed, with a cigarette lighter tucked into the front of her green and white pareo (a wraparound skirt that's cousin to the sarong), was the driver for a mini-bus tour around the island that I took with a half-dozen other visitors. "You can't pronounce my real name," she said. "So, just call me Sugar."

As we drove past Matira Beach, we could see out beyond the lagoon to the sandy, palm-covered islets (known as motu) that form part of the barrier reef and where many of the luxury hotels now stand.

One of the other passengers wanted to know if people lived on the motu. No, Sugar said, families usually went out there for only a few days at a time to gather coconuts.

"How romantic," said the woman, who, like seemingly half the tourists on the island, was on her honeymoon.

Sugar turned and looked at the woman as if she were as dumb as a land crab. "Coconuts is hard work. I did coconuts, stooping over all day to pick them up. It's hard for your back. As soon as I passed my license, I say the heck with these things, I'm staying with the bus."

We drove counter-clockwise around the island, along the lagoon-hugging road that was another gift of the U.S. military. On the inland side, a single row of thatched or tin-roof houses backed up against the green skirts of the ancient, twin-peaked volcanic cone that dominates the island. As we drove, it seemed that much house building was going on. They looked like traditional houses, framed with straight, thin tree trunks so recently stripped of their bark that they were still freshly white.

"No, not houses," said Sugar, in a tone that made me suspect she might think that the woman on her honeymoon wasn't the only one as dumb as a land crab.

The structures were temporary food, liquor, and games-of-chance stalls being erected for Bastille Day, which the Tahitians had stretched into a month-long celebration that was often the setting for, as one Bora Boran told me, "The year's best feuds and romances."

Toward the end of our tour—from the old Club Med that closed following a December 1991 hurricane, all the way around to Bloody Mary's, an American-run bar whose varnished wooden tote board of celebrity visitors was proof that name dropping could be an art—we could see the sailing cruise ship *Wind Song* riding at anchor in the lagoon.

Back at the Hotel Bora Bora, one of the managers, an American named Al Robbs, told me that a few years earlier, one of the passengers aboard the *Wind Song* had been James A. Michener. While on the island, Michener was taken by sailing canoe across the lagoon for a birthday lunch at the hotel.

"He told me," said Al, 'You are living the life I always dreamed of living."

To me, too, it seemed like Bora Bora could be a dream life, at least for a while. Who wouldn't want to spend an afternoon in a hammock in front of a thatched-roof bungalow? Or ride a bicycle to a roadside stand where the proprietor would use his machete to lop off the top of a drinking coconut for you? Or canoe out to a reef, where you could swim in chest-deep water among sharks as they were hand-fed by locals skilled at convincing you that you were in absolutely no danger?

And it seemed that some Americans—a group usually numbering around fifteen or sixteen—had found ways to live the dream life on Bora Bora more or less permanently. Most of these long-staying Americans had established residency by marrying Bora Borans (the most straightforward way, if you didn't have a needed job skill, to circumvent the strict French laws about how long foreigners could stay). Most had golden-skinned children who were more Polynesian than American. And most considered Bora Bora, more than America, their home.

But as someone who had made a career of escaping attachments whenever possible, no matter how pleasant the circumstances, I wondered if they really were living a dream life. When you live on Bora Bora, is it paradise? Or is it just where you live?

To find out, I talked with expatriates such as Robin Teraaitepo, an American who had been living on Bora Bora for five years with her Tahitian husband, Ben.

"When I was growing up in Oklahoma," Robin told me, "the closest I ever thought I was going to get to paradise was watching *The Don Ho Show*. And look at me now."

And I talked with locals, ranging from the mayor, who had recently come to power on the promise of running water for every home, to a young Bora Boran male who had returned from a visit to California with the belief that American women were much easier to live with than Tahitian women. "American woman, to show her you love her, you just buy flowers. Bora Boran woman, that don't work."

My conclusion was that Bora Bora is paradise. But for an outsider, living in paradise is not easy. You have to work hard at understanding the people among whom you have chosen to live. And you have to work hard at understanding yourself.

You have to understand that pureblooded Bora Borans, unlike your own unfortunate self, are not the product of a cold-weather culture where the idea of getting ahead developed as a necessity for surviving the winter. To them, the chief attraction of a job is often the opportunity to visit with friends.

You have to understand, when you see a Bora Boran throw a can or a bottle on the ground, that until not too long ago, when the outside world brought cans and bottles, the elements saw to it that anything they dropped on the ground quickly rotted and disappeared.

You have to understand, when you hear that it is relatively common for a Bora Boran man to beat his wife "because a

Bora Boran woman does not respect a man who does not physically dominate her," that there is much about our own society we don't understand either.

You have to understand that in all these matters, Bora Borans, like people everywhere, resent having someone come in from the outside and try to tell them how things ought to be done in their own country. "All you can do," said Richard Postma, "is set an example."

As a resident of paradise, you have to understand that you will always be on stage. Nothing about your life on the island will be unknown or un-discussed. You will not, as Al Robbs said he sometimes wished he could, be able to get in an automobile and drive until you reach a place where no one knows you.

You have to understand that if you stay long enough, you might discover that you have nowhere else to go. "Can you imagine me trying to get a job someplace in the States, with a twenty-five-year lapse in my curriculum vitae?" said Keith Olsen, a middle-aged North Dakotan who had been in Polynesia since he was a teenager.

And finally, you have to understand that no matter how hard you try to come to terms with paradise, you will probably not succeed as well as an outsider named Alfred Doom.

Alfred, a Tahitian with American blood, arrived on Bora Bora from Tahiti in 1948 aboard a ship on which he worked. When he arrived, he had only the pair of pants he was wearing the night he went ashore to visit an island girl. He stayed so late visiting the girl that the ship—the freighter that made a monthly circuit of the Society Islands—sailed without him. Forty-five years later, he was still on Bora Bora and still married to the same girl.

"Bora Bora is very calm when I first come," said Alfred. "Few bicycles, some horses, and lot of canoe. The canoe then is like the scooter today. And the old way of fishing and coconuts is still OK then."

But as the years went on, the traditional way of life seemed less OK to Alfred and less OK to his wife, whose family is Chinese. In the late 1950s, he went to New Caledonia to work in the nickel mines and came home with enough money to buy the island's third automobile, a DeSoto.

At the time, it would have been hard to imagine any purchase more extravagant or useless than an automobile on Bora Bora. Unless, of course, you were Alfred Doom and had the imagination to see the possibilities created in 1961, when the island's first resort, the Hotel Bora Bora, began attracting tourists to its thatched-roof bungalows that sat beneath the palm trees beside the most beautiful lagoon in the world.

In the beginning, the Hotel Bora Bora owned a jeep. But there were days when the jeep was unable to handle all the transportation needs of the guests. On those days, the hotel hired Alfred. "In the beginning, I am the spare tire," he said.

By the time I met him, when he was sixty-two, he was the big wheel. Mr. Transportation. Mr. Member of the Tourism Committee. Mr. Uncle of the New Mayor. He had lived happily. He had prospered. And he had thought as much as anyone about the future of his adopted paradise.

He worried about commercial boats coming from elsewhere to take fish from the waters of Bora Bora. "You fishing for your family, OK. You eat the fish, as much as you want, OK. You make money, no. These fish are for this island."

He had thought about plans for building more hotels on Bora Bora, which had fewer hotel rooms (about 400 at that time, compared to twice that when I last visited) than a single medium-size hotel in Hawaii. And he was in favor of such plans. Up to a point. "Make hotels until all people on island who want hotel job have one. We don't want people come from other island for job."

He had considered the possibility that French Polynesia

could become an independent nation. "The majority, they want to be independent, but they know we not ready. We better stay with the French for the moment. Maybe twenty years, maybe more, maybe. But for the moment—no."

French Polynesia was not ready for independence, he said, because it was not ready to stand on its own financially.

As we watched a group of Japanese tourists spend a scheduled thirty minutes sitting on the beach, I asked him what might allow French Polynesia to stand on its own financially.

His answer was that of a man who deserves to live in an island paradise and always be happy there.

"Maybe we can find a way," he said, "to make smiles grow on trees."

10
Food Writer? Martinique? You Bet!

Not long after the Bora Bora story appeared in *Islands* magazine, I got an e-mail from the executive editor at *Bon Appétit* magazine, Barbara Fairchild.

According to *Islands* editor Joan Tapper, Barbara had read the Bora Bora story and was impressed with my insightful critique of canned corn beef. (Perhaps I do not remember this part exactly right.)

Barbara asked me if I spoke French, and I answered, as any freelancer should, no matter what the language, "Just enough to get me in trouble."

And she wanted to know if I'd like to go to Martinique.

I immediately said yes, of course. But as it happened, I did have some unvoiced reservations about doing the story. I recognize that for many people, food is a reason to travel, maybe the most important reason. But despite even my stint as the cook for a crew of women aboard an ocean-going sailboat, I am not a foodie. I once lived in an apartment for six weeks before discovering the stove wasn't hooked up. And my understanding of wine is that the second bottle almost always tastes better than the first.

But the possibility of a byline in *Bon Appétit* was not something to be ignored. And one of the fundamental requirements for being a journalist is the ability to write on any subject. It's just a matter of asking enough questions—and getting the answers recorded so that someone can later explain what is really being said. So, I took the assignment, for the first of maybe a dozen stories I wrote for them. I enjoyed working with Barbara, and I learned a bit about food, including that some dishes, turtle stew, for example, which I tried in the Cayman Islands, should be saved for special occasions, such as if you find yourself adrift in a life raft.

* * *

My introduction to Martinique began at a table so close to the sand that I could plainly see what fashionable French women were not wearing to the beach that year. In my mind, I judged the crabes farcis (stuffed crab) I was starting lunch with to be too peppery. But in the interest of fairness and journalism, I solicited a second opinion, from my taxi driver, who was dining with me. "Good," she said, "But not enough pepper."

The driver, Bernadette Ductiel, who was five months pregnant with her fifth child, had, when I got into her cab at the airport, offered me her services as a guide. And her quick, sure judgment about the crabs not only convinced me that I had found a talented critic but also made me begin to suspect something that, by the end of my stay, I would be confident of.

In the finest French tradition, Martinique is an island where people love to talk about food even more than they love to talk about politics. And on Martinique, if there is one thing they agree about, it is that to eat food the way it is meant to be eaten, you can't forget the pepper. By which they mean hot, spicy chili pepper.

"Oh goodness no," said a local epicure I accidentally tripped over a few days later as he napped in the shade of a red, yellow, and blue fishing boat pulled up on the beach at Anses-d'Arlets. "It's no good without the pepper."

Martinique's food is Creole, sometimes with a touch of

Indian, but said to be prepared with a mastery that only an island steeped in French culture could bring to the table. A typical dish was accras, which are fritters made with fish or, occasionally, vegetables. They were offered to me everywhere I went, usually accompanied, "to open your appetite," by the traditional island drink, ti-punch, which consists of one part sugar cane syrup to four parts white rum.

The art of eating accras is in being able to judge, by experience, the exact instant to pop one whole into your mouth and bite down on it slowly until the hard crust collapses into the softer center, letting the flavor and just the right amount of heat flow together into your mouth and—if you've mastered the art—your soul.

And if, as would sometimes happen, the accras are so big that you risk bringing attention to yourself by attempting to eat them in one bite, the fault is not with your manners but with the chef's method.

I did attract attention at one restaurant, Le Fromager. However, it wasn't because of the accras but the number of paper towels I went through before I became comfortable with the proper barehanded technique for getting the most enjoyment out of colombo d'ecrevisses, an island-grown crayfish in a blend of Indian spices.

"No, no, not the fork, the fingers," the waiter told me as I accidentally propelled an ecrevisse across a clean tablecloth. Accras, I concluded, made a much more sensible finger food than ecrevisses.

Not that I spent the entire week thinking only about accras. I also gave considerable attention to rum.

* * *

I should first point out that I am more familiar than most with that particular drink because I consider myself a sailor, and rum—dark rum preferably, Mount Gay if you have it—is a sailor's drink. Unless the sailor is in Bermuda, where they will be drinking Gosling's and ginger beer, the combination being well known, in Bermuda, as a Dark 'n Stormy.

Other than that sailors never wear socks with their boat shoes, even at funerals and weddings, the easiest way to identify them is by what they mix their rum with: tonic, except in Bermuda, and a wedge of lime, not a twist, and not a slice, unless they imagine themselves to be old-time tall-ship sailors. Then, it will be equal parts rum and water—the drink otherwise known as grog.

I have come across many bartenders who were ignorant of any of this. From which I have always concluded that I was too far from the sea.

But I wander.

* * *

On Martinique, my thoughts about rum began at Le Fromager, located on a mountainside overlooking what's left of Saint-Pierre, the one-time capital of Martinique, whose population of 30,000 was wiped out in less than three minutes early one morning in 1902, when Mount Pelee erupted. To temper the spices of Le Fromager's colombo d'ecrevisses, I followed it with a banana flambee and a glass of straight rum. The rum was rhum vieux, old rum, dark gold and having a flavor reminiscent of fine brandy.

I thought about that rum (warm, pleasant, glowing thoughts) as we headed north from Saint-Pierre, skirting the base of Mount Pelee. Rolling past fields of sugar cane, pineapples, and bananas, we finally came to the wild north coast between Basse-Pointe and Grand'Riviere, where jungle waterfalls cascaded alongside—and, sometimes, during the rainy season, onto—the twisting mountain road.

I continued to think about it after we arrived in Grand'Riviere, where I had planned to open up my appetite by walking for a mile or so along the rugged coastal footpath that is one of Martinique's officially marked hiking trails. But considering my guide Bernadette's condition and not wanting to run the risk of a pregnant woman outpacing me, I opted instead to visit the Museum of Rum.

The museum was on the east side of Martinique, in the town of Sainte-Marie. It was run by the Plantations Saint James distillery, largest of the fourteen distilleries that remained in operation from the more than 200 whose crumbling brick chimneys, ancient, rusting machinery, and witches-brew-like cauldrons could still be seen all over the island.

"The good rum comes from cane grown in the good, volcanic soil," said a guide who took me on a brief museum tour that ended in the tasting room. I supposed he should know, as the original Saint James distillery, located near Saint-Pierre, disappeared beneath the good volcanic soil of Mount Pelee during the 1902 eruption.

Between them, St. James and its chief rival, La Mauny, accounted for a majority of the rum produced on Martinique. Yet when I talked with some people who considered themselves to be rum experts (three aging sugar cane cutters with whom I fell into conversation in La Savane, the main square and park in the heart of Martinique's capital city, Fort-de-France), they said that to meet demand St. James and La Mauny seemed to rush the process a bit. The cane cutters all agreed that for people who truly appreciate the taste of rum, the smaller distilleries produced a more satisfying product. What they couldn't agree on was which small distillery produced the *most* satisfying.

* * *

This gave a focus to my remaining days on Martinique, when I attempted to discover for myself the most satisfying rum.

My quest was aided immensely by the fact that most distilleries, no matter how small, encouraged visitors and rewarded them with a degustation gratuite, a free tasting. Wandering off from the guided tour at one distillery and admiring with a nod the efficiency with which a worker was turning some valves, I even got a taste of "baby rum." Fresh out of the still and as clear as spring water, it was so potent that just one sip was enough to make me agree wholeheartedly with the observation of the grinning worker: "The baby rum, it kicks the hardest."

The thought of all that kicking made me realize that for my quest to have any hope of success, I would have to pace myself, just as if I were walking a long trail up the side of a mountain. I did it by making sure I devoted sufficient time to the island's other sights and pleasures.

Among them, I looked out to sea at Diamond Rock, which once served as a fully manned and fully armed British warship, a warship that was finally defeated in battle only after the French floated barrels of Martinique rum out to the thirsty crew. And I visited the Pagerie museum, on the grounds of the ruined sugar estate that was the birthplace of Marie Josephe Rose Tascher de la Pagerie, better known as Napoleon's Empress Josephine.

My favorite exhibit at the museum was a love letter that seemed to indicate just how little Napoleon, one of the world's greatest military strategists, understood about winning with women. "I am sending you a piece of taffeta," he had written Josephine. "Do you see how generous I am? This has cost me more than thirty pounds."

One of my most enjoyable pleasures was walking. I walked the white sands of the beach at Les Salines. I walked through the high, central rainforest, where every step brought me to a reminder of why the Carib Indians had called Martinique the "Island of Flowers." And I walked the narrow, balconied streets of Fort-de-France, where I marveled at the Schoelcher Library, an imposing rococo-style structure built for the Paris Exposition of 1889, dismantled, then shipped to the island with—one hopes—instructions for reassembly.

I took time out to visit some of the island's hotels, inns, and more than 150 restaurants, discovering that among my favorite dishes were callaloo, a soup made with vegetables, herbs, salted pork, sea crabs, and blaff, the latter being a style of poached fish.

"Blaff?" answered a woman I shared a bench with on the ferry between Fort-de-France and a marina near my hotel. "You put your water on the fire. You put in all your seasonings. Then when your water starts boiling, you put in your fish. The fish makes a sound—blaff."

I never did determine the island's single most satisfying rum. Despite my diligence, and the willingness of many people to assist me in my quest by offering their own opinions, I could only narrow it down to my favorite four: Bally, Clement, Favorite, and J.M.

I did come away from Martinique convinced of one thing, though. Just before departing, I stopped for lunch with Bernadette at a nondescript place near the airport that catered to tourists. Their red snapper fillet was OK, I thought, but it needed more pepper.

11
Headhunters Laughed at What I Paid for My Wife

In 1993, one of my sailing friends, an American named Nick Ellison, asked if I'd help him get his boat from Darwin, in Australia, across the Indian Ocean to the Seychelles.

He was on a voyage around the world, and except for one other friend, whose eagerness to accompany him was possibly related to a lack of understanding of what might be involved, he could find no one else who wanted to do that leg.

There was the distance, almost 5,000 nautical miles, which would mean about a month at sea, most of it out of sight of land. There was the possibility, although a bit late in the season for it, of cyclones. And there was some concern, not for the first time in my sailing career, about pirates.

I said yes, immediately. Then, to pay for the trip and better justify a journey that overall could take almost three months, I scrambled to come up with writing assignments in that part of the world.

The one I got that intrigued me the most, for *Islands* magazine, would take me to Nias, an Indonesian island off the west coast of Sumatra whose people were so late in coming out of the Stone Age that some of their megalithic carvings were of steamships.

Admittedly, some 2,500 miles from Darwin, Nias was not exactly "in that part of the world." Especially since adding it to my itinerary required stopovers in Singapore and Bali and several overnight bus rides through Sumatra and Java.

But I knew the extra effort was worth it when, on one of the bus rides, I observed with admiration the skill with which somebody picked my pocket. And on another, to the Sumatran port town of Sibolga, I sat in the very back of the bus, atop burlap sacks filled with sharp-edged pots and pans, while an Indonesian woman who was wedged in next to me kept saying, "You give me your address, I write you in America."

I was even more convinced I'd made the right decision when, on the overnight ferry from Sibolga to Nias, an Indonesian man questioned me about my interest in what I guessed must be the mortuary statues for which the island was famous. "You come," he asked, "for the big right-handers?"

Helpfully, too, during the sixty-mile open-water crossing, I was able to gather a clearer picture of the island from an Austrian backpacker who was visiting it for the third time in as many years.

The Austrian, who I'd first noticed when I heard him attempting to explain to unconvinced Indonesians that Australia was an entirely different place from his homeland, said that to immerse myself in Nias one step at a time, I ought to begin at the coastal village of Lagundi.

The village possessed few examples of primitive culture, he said, unless you counted the Australian surfers there for the big right-handed waves. But it did have a beautiful beach, where, beneath the palm trees at the edge of the sand, you could rent a bungalow for one U.S. dollar a day.

Skilled bargainers could do even better, he said, just as long as they kept in mind that they were dealing with people who had been headhunters as recently as the 1930s.

Although the Nias people, as they called themselves, were now considered peaceful, devout Christians, their reputation as fierce headhunters, the Austrian told me, helped isolate the island and allow its megalithic culture to remain relatively undisturbed well into the 20th century.

Apparently, 1935 was the last year in which head-hunting occurred on Nias, ending a tradition that had been going on at least since A.D. 851, when an Arab merchant who had visited the island wrote that for a man on Nias to take a wife, he first had to take another man's head.

"Now, a man must first go to Jakarta or Medan and earn the bride price," the Austrian said. "Sometimes as much as five thousand American dollars. It must make some of those fellows miss the old days, yah?"

* * *

Not long after sunrise, Nias' green sharp-edged hills, fresh-washed from a tropical rain shower, appeared off the ferry's bow. We landed at Teluk Dalam, which had been the main port for the south end of the island ever since a tsunami from the 1883 explosion of Krakatoa wiped out the port at Lagundi Bay.

A dozen years after my visit, in 2004, Nias would again be hit by a tsunami, the same one that decimated coastal communities all around the Indian Ocean. And a few months after that, it would find itself not far from the epicenter of one of the most powerful earthquakes Indonesia has ever recorded. The result was more than a thousand deaths on Nias, and the destruction, according to reports, of much of the island's infrastructure.

The latter information particularly caught my attention because I couldn't recall seeing, during my visit, much infrastructure to begin with. In fact, I remember wondering, as I rode on the back of a motorbike from Teluk Dalam to Lagundi, if there was any infrastructure at all.

Hired motorbike was the standard transport to Lagundi, typically one that looked as if it had been involved in several accidents and numerous incidents of mudslinging. Along with me on my motorbike were my bag, a driver, whose name was

Aturan, and Aturan's business associate, who called himself Eddy. Both men were small and wiry and, to my amazement, could sing the first verse of "Wake Up Little Suzie," a song by the 1950s American pop duo the Everly Brothers, which they said they'd learned at school, in English class.

The ride was like sitting in the front car of a roller coaster, except that you are reasonably confident the roller coaster isn't going to spin off into a palm tree. At a breakneck ten miles per hour, we traveled along a rain-slick, pot-holed surface that may or may not have been a road. We traveled through rice fields, across jungle rivers, and past people using huge leaves as umbrellas, until we came at last to a beautiful palm-lined bay.

We arrived at the bay, Lagundi, just as the sun came out and sent steam spiraling up from every surface. Along the shore were about two-dozen small, basic, thatched-roof inns known throughout Indonesia as losmen. All the losmen consisted of a handful of detached or haphazardly attached bungalows.

Although Aturan and Eddy lobbied hard for me to stay at a losmen they swore they had no business connection with, my first choice was a place called the Risky, which appealed to me because of its name. (Risky turned out to be the family's firstborn son, his name suggested to them by a no-doubt culturally irresponsible European who had been in residence when the child was born.) But a group of Dutch travelers had claimed all the beds at the Risky, so I hefted my bag and walked barefoot down the beach in search of something else.

Accompanied by an entourage of chattering kids trying to sell me bananas, pineapples, fish, woodcarvings, and photo opportunities, I finally came to the Losmen Yanty, where I spotted a bungalow with a sea-view front porch that I had to have.

Mr. Milyar, who had named the losmen after his daughter Yanty, had a winning smile and drove a hard bargain. He pointed out that because my bungalow was one of the few on the beach with a private mandi (distant cousin to the Western bathroom), I would need to pay a premium. But we finally agreed on a price of 2,500 rupiahs a night ($1.25), with the understanding that I would also eat my meals there. Meals, I saw from the menu, could add as much as another two dollars to the daily tab.

Most of the megaliths on Nias are located in the traditional villages at the island's south end, in the hills above Lagundi. I had intended to head for them after only a night at the Losmen Yanty. But I found Lagundi so appealing that I stayed several days and contemplated staying even longer—perhaps a year, or two.

I walked the beach, especially at mid-morning when the fishermen in their brightly decorated outrigger sailing canoes returned with the day's catch. I contracted with a nine-year-old fruit vendor to supply me, for fifty cents a day, with a daily pineapple and a bunch of bananas that I hung from the roof beams for when friends dropped by in an attempt to sell me more. I stood on the point and watched a handful of surfers handle or be handled by what they claimed, in surf speak, were some of the best right-handed waves in Indonesia.

I briefly speculated on how much Mr. Milyar might drop his rate if I would commit to a long-term lease.

Eventually, though, because a travel writer must travel (or at least did in the days before there was a nearly limitless selection of online images one could appropriate, with or without giving credit), I set out for the traditional villages. And for reasons that Singapore founder Sir Thomas Stamford Raffles would have understood, I went on foot.

* * *

When Raffles, searching for new worlds to colonize after Singapore, visited Nias in the early 1800s, he said, "...the interior surpasses in beauty and fertility the richest parts of continental

India, if not of Java."

Yet despite Raffles' enthusiasm, Nias never became a British colony. One reason was that travel to the interior of Nias, where the traditional villages are located, was extremely difficult during his day. At the time of my visit, even before the destruction of much of the island's alleged infrastructure by the most recent tsunami and earthquake, interior travel was easier, but only marginally.

So, even though you could reach some villages by frequently washed-out roads, often requiring detours around bridges that had collapsed or looked like they were about to, most traffic within the interior remained foot traffic.

Accompanying me on my walking journey was a guide I hired, Kadis, who claimed to be seventeen years old and said he had relatives in the village of Hilinawalo who would put us up for the night. Diminutive even by Indonesian standards, Kadis wore baggy blue jeans rolled up many times at the cuffs and was the proud owner of a pair of walking shoes on which the word Reebok was spelled with only one "e."

Kadis was an agreeable companion, and his English wasn't too bad, although much of it consisted of Australian surf speak and the sentence, "Now you want to buy a statue?"

Despite being adjacent to a road, the village of Hilisimaetano, where we started our walk, was typical of the half dozen traditional villages we would pass through during the next several days. It consisted of two long, facing rows of attached stilt houses, separated by a stone-paved courtyard that, to some ways of thinking, cried out for a couple of basketball hoops.

The houses—looking something like the ornate stern castles of ancient sailing ships, which were apparently their design inspiration—were built well off the ground on thick timbers and capped by high, sharp-peaked roofs. Kadis said that traditionally the timbers were driven into the ground only after someone's head had been planted beneath them. "Brings good luck, except for the man the head belongs to," he said.

In front of the houses, the courtyard was lined with megaliths: stone altars, headstone-like obelisks, and king-size stone benches, tables, and chairs. Some were smooth grey, some intricately carved with designs of birds, animals, flowers, and such man-made objects as ancient swords and pistols.

Among the more curious objects was a six-foot-high stone pyramid used for stone jumping, a still-practiced warrior-training ritual similar to the Western sport of high jumping, except that the consequences of not making it over the top are infinitely more painful. On the chance that I didn't understand this, Kadis illustrated it for me by grabbing his crotch and groaning in feigned agony.

Where Nias' megalithic culture originated is generally considered a mystery. Some scholars think it came from India, some from the hill tribes of Burma. But the more intriguing theories pointed to the similarities between the stonework of Nias and other prehistoric megalithic sites around the world, ranging from Stonehenge to Easter Island.

The theories also pointed to the fact that the language of Nias is strikingly different from other Indonesian languages, being in some respects similar to Polynesian.

Kadis had no theory about where Nias culture came from. Nor did he know what other languages the language of Nias might be related to.

"But I am wishing one is English," he said, with an eye to his statue sales.

* * *

From Hilisimaetano, we headed through the countryside along a slippery stone path that I imagined had been laid out by some prehistoric highway department. The path led upward, often so steeply that the stones became steps. Sometimes, we traveled through shadowy, humid stands of forest, sometimes, through bright, hot clearings planted with taro, maize, and sweet potatoes. Several times, we worked our way down and then up the other side of a jungle-covered ravine. And once, we crossed a rock-strewn river on a bridge of logs.

Occasionally, we would be overtaken by sweating young men with straining ropes of muscle in their legs and an ox-like crossbar balanced over their shoulders. At each end of the bar hung a sack of supplies for the uphill villages that could be reached by no other means of transport.

Kadis exchanged pleasantries with all the men and taught me to say "Yaho'wu," a traditional Nias greeting that means "strength." I made especially sure to use it when we stopped to rest alongside a stream in the company of three rough-looking hunters who put down their spears and bush knives to take time out for a smoke.

At the villages, we would climb a set of stone stairs and find ourselves in the long, stone-terraced courtyard, its sun-baked surface often covered with squares of drying rice and patchouli leaves. In the more prosperous villages, some sections of stone looked as if they had been smoothed over with concrete. The high, slanted roofs of the courtyard houses were made of thatch or, more commonly, corrugated tin. Visitors such as myself usually didn't like the tin, Kadis told me, but it cut down considerably on the risk of losing an entire village to fire.

The village we stayed in, Hilinawalo, was the most traditional in appearance. However, our lodging was a two-story cement block structure representing the "Chinese" style said to be favored by the nouveau riche, among whose Kadis' relatives apparently numbered. What made the lodging special, though, was the view from the second-story balcony.

Beginning at lunch, while Kadis and I ate mie goring, or fried noodles, spiced to a degree that made it obvious the lady of the house had not compromised her standards to meet the tastes of the tourist trade, I was able to sit for hours and unobtrusively observe Nias village life.

I watched a group of women sitting in the shade of the houses, catching up on village gossip and, listlessly or energetically, as the situation demanded, chucking stones at chickens whose itinerant scratching brought them into the territory of the women's patches of drying rice or patchouli.

I watched men whose village responsibilities seemed to require a considerable amount of chess playing. And I watched little boys form a line of attack, then, with grimaces, shouts, and raised wooden spears, charge imaginary foes.

When the growing shadows from the high roofs began to cover the courtyard, I watched families of pigs, who on Nias held a place of honor, come out from under the houses and wander around with the royal manner that was their right.

Although pork-abhorring Muslims populate most of Indonesia, the people of Nias, the majority of them now Christians, had traditionally based their economy largely on pig farming. The economy was shifting toward growing rice and other crops, and there were the beginnings of a tourism industry. But significant financial transactions, including determining a bride price, were still often reckoned in pigs.

Which is why, in the evening, when Kadis and I sat in front of the house with the "Papa," as he called him, and a son-in-law, and a couple of young men from the neighborhood, the topic of our conversations was always the same.

As we sat on a stone bench under which the skulls of ancestors used to be placed so that their spirits would be close at hand whenever someone felt the need to consult them, we were talking, Kadis told me, about how many pigs various passing village maidens would be able to command as a bride price.

"How many pigs you pay for your wife?" he asked me at the request of one of the young men. And he set them atwitter when he translated that where I came from, the island called America, the man had to give only a tiny band worn around the woman's finger, and not even her biggest finger.

When it was completely dark, the "Momma" came out with a gas lantern. As she hung the lantern on a hook above the door, I noticed the wiring for an electric light. Kadis said the village had electricity, but that it had not been working for either two months or two years. No one seemed to remember which.

In the light of the lantern, the son-in-law produced a guitar. His playing soon gathered a crowd, including three young girls who accompanied him with pleasant, harmonious voices. I thought we might be in for quite a party, especially when Kadis went somewhere to purchase, at my expense, two bottles of red wine that captured exactly the flavor of children's cherry-flavored cough syrup.

But then Kadis convinced me that the crowd wanted to hear me sing. And after one chorus of the only song I knew well enough to get all the way through in front of strangers—"Happy Birthday"—the party broke up, the girls and the brother-in-law claiming they had choir practice to attend.

* * *

In the morning, I awoke to a fragrance that, with some considerable distance from it, I have ever after remembered with nostalgic fondness. It was the fragrance of cooking fires and pig excrement.

After a breakfast of sweet potatoes and tea, Kadis and I hiked down through the villages of Onohondo and Siwalawa. Both looked a bit run down, or so I judged by the amount of grass growing between the stones in their courtyard. But our final village, Bawomataluo, was entirely different. The main village on the road that ran up from Teluk Dalam, it had what could only be described as a grandly prosperous air.

In Bawomataluo, no grass grew between the cracks, roofs were being repaired, and timbers were being cut for new doorframes. Bottled soft drinks were offered for sale. And a half dozen people spoke to me in English, although, admittedly, in every case, their side of the conversation was mostly limited to, "Allo mister."

What, I asked Kadis, had brought such seemingly good fortune to Bawomataluo? Was it the quality of the nearly 300 stone sculptures that lined the courtyard? Was it the magnificence of the chief's house, whose rooftop soared sixty feet above the village? Was it the reputation of the village's stone jumpers, or its dancers, who were acclaimed for their acrobatic feats?

In answer, he led me to the chief's house and, after some wrangling, secured an invitation for us to go inside. Climbing a set of steps past wooden beams that were three feet thick, we entered a dark, cool room, obviously used for the formal reception of visitors. And there, on the wall, was revealed the secret of Bawomataluo's prosperity. In a place of honor, where shrunken heads no doubt used to reside, and where no visitor could fail to gaze upon it, hung a framed photograph of a cruise ship.

12

In the Seychelles
Every Position is Paintable

After Nias and a side trip to Bali and Lombok, again by bus and ferry, I flew to Darwin, at the top of Australia. Arriving at 3 a.m., I found my sailing friend Nick Ellison waiting for me at the airport with, as was usually the case, a bit of off-color doggerel, this one ending, "So I bucked one and Timbuktu."

Nick was a real-estate developer who lived on the banks of the Ohio River in Fort Thomas, Kentucky. And, like more than a few people I knew, he had dreamed for much of his life of a voyage around the world. The dream intensified after his first job interview, with a bank in Cincinnati, when they told him they wouldn't hire him because he had diabetes. Which they said would keep him from doing the traveling the job required.

Decades after the interview, he still had to carry insulin and other diabetic supplies wherever he went. There was a special shelf for them in the aft cabin of his boat. And next to the hatch that led into the cockpit, there was always an orange emergency bag with additional diabetic necessities, should some disaster occur that required instantly abandoning ship. But his voyage was one more example of how his condition had never held him back and how fortunate we who sailed with him were that a bank in Cincinnati had been so short-sighted.

Nick and I had sailed together aboard his boat, *Lusty Wind*, in the Bahamas, when he was getting ready for the voyage, and I was writing a story for *Sail* about his preparations.

We'd gotten along so well that we later co-authored a book, *The International Marine Boat Manager*, whose annual sales peaked, I think, at around twelve copies.

The book wasn't a riveting read. "Your Vessel's Custom Handbook of Operating and Service Procedures," the subtitle proclaimed, which is probably as far as most readers got. But I recall it for two reasons.

One is that more than twenty-five years later, McGraw-Hill still makes a royalty payment to me every six months. And I wonder, each time I get it, how much workforce, paper, ink, and postage were expended in creating my check for—the most recent was a typical amount—$1.08.

The other is what happened during the voyage as we approached Cocos Keeling, a tiny group of twenty-seven coral islands on two atolls in the Indian Ocean, about 1,500 miles west of Darwin. The place has a surprisingly interesting history, including that it is where Charles Darwin, aboard the *Beagle*, would make the observations that helped him put together his theory on the formation of coral atolls. And it also has, as we discovered, a surprisingly tricky entrance by sea.

We'd made landfall in the early hours of the morning, long before sunrise. The seas were running high, and we could hear breakers pounding on the encircling reef. As you always do when approaching a strange shore for the first time, especially in the dark, especially amid coral, we felt uncertain. And to make it worse, the lights that were supposed to lead us into the safety of the lagoon seemed all wrong.

"What do you think we should do?" I asked Nick.

"I don't know," he answered. "What did we say in the book?"

But other than our confused but ultimately successful arrival at Cocos Keeling (we did what we were supposed to and waited until dawn, when we discovered that an anchored fishing vessel had been blocking some of the lights we were looking for), the voyage was what the old tall-ship sailors would have called a flying-fish run. Which is like a milk run, but without the milk. Seventeen days out of Cocos Keeling, we sighted Frigate Island, in the Seychelles, and a few days later, soon after signing off *Lusty Wind*, I was afloat again, in the pursuit of my next writing assignment.

* * *

In the pink-and-purple light of a perfect Seychelles dawn, I was aboard the forty-foot sailing catamaran *King Bamboo*, and we were running under full sail before a brisk monsoon breeze.

"She feels good, no?" said skipper Eugene Aspa, who seemed untroubled by the gender mixing or by our actual progress.

Even with the aid of our twin auxiliary diesel engines, we were moving at a rate of no more than four knots, less than half the speed I'd often experienced aboard *Lusty Wind*. It was a speed that, by comparison, would have made even the slowest boat to China feel like the *Shanghai Express*. The boat actually felt like it was dragging a dead whale. But you couldn't say that to a man blinded by pride. Besides, Eugene's two crew members seemed equally unconcerned by our lack of progress.

Maxime Telemaque, who we called Tele, was spooling out the heavy fishing lines we trailed astern when the boat was underway during daylight hours. All Seychellois seemed to be expert fishermen. But it wouldn't be long before Tele would display his special talent: flipping a kingfish or mackerel out of the sea and into a simmering Creole sauce before the creature even noticed that the water was becoming uncomfortably warm.

John Benoiton, who was looking less lost than at any other time since we'd left the harbor at Victoria, on the main island of Mahe, two days earlier, had just finished his most recent effort at determining *King Bamboo*'s position with the sextant. (This was in the days before GPS made it possible to know where you are at all times, even if where you ought to be is ashore.) I believe his effort had finally indicated we were in the Indian Ocean. Satisfied, he had gone back to sleep on the settee in the main salon.

I confess I was not much troubled by our slow progress either. After I departed *Lusty Wind*, the Seychelles Tourism Board had insisted I make use of *King Bamboo* and her crew for a few days of exploring the Seychelles. And even having just sailed halfway across the Indian Ocean, I could not imagine a more pleasant way to see the islands. Nor could I imagine that getting quickly from one of them to another should have anything to do with it.

Still, our goal that morning was Bird Island, which ocean currents were sweeping into the sea at up to thirty feet a year. And I did want to get there before it was gone.

Bird, a Robinson Crusoe kind of place, is one of the 115 islands that make up the Seychelles, a remote island group not far from the equator and not near much of anything else. They are a thousand miles east of Africa, in a quiet part of the Indian Ocean where the sun almost always shines, and tropical cyclones almost never blow. The sun and the remoteness, not to mention the abundance of palm-lined beaches (among them one that numerous travelers have ranked as the most beautiful in the world), had made the Seychelles one of those island sanctuaries—like Bali and Bora Bora—that people think of as an earthly paradise.

There was once a seriously proposed theory that the Seychelles was the site of the Garden of Eden. The theory was not entirely dead, especially among tourists waiting for the long flights back to Europe or, less frequently, America. How better, they asked, to explain the Seychelles' most famous fruit, a unique type of coconut often referred to, because of its suggestive shape, as the love nut? And how better to explain that the people of the Seychelles, mostly Creoles with a well-blended mix of African, European, Indian, and Arab blood, were so at ease with racial harmony and having children out of wedlock?

Geologically, the Seychelles can be divided into two distinct groups. One group is the forty-one high and softly rounded granite islands that make the Seychelles unique. Remnants of the ancient southern super-continent Gondwanaland (which gave birth to South America, Africa, Madagascar, and India), they are the world's only mid-ocean granite islands. Like an exclusive inner circle, they sit together within sight of each other on the Seychelles Bank.

Near the circle's center is Mahe, the largest and most populated of the islands and the one where the few big (relatively speaking) hotels were. It was the island where tourists splashed happily in the waters of Beau Vallon Beach. Or wandered afoot across lush hillsides or through one of the world's smallest capital cities, Victoria, where they were perhaps too polite to ask if the sculpture in the middle of the roundabout just past the Cable & Wireless station was supposed to look like two fishtails sticking out of the ground.

On the fringe of the inner circle of granite islands, and looking very much like an uninvited guest, is Bird Island. Bird is one of the Seychelles' seventy-four coral islands, spread out over more than 150,000 square miles of ocean. It is one of only two coral islands to share the Seychelles Bank with the granite islands. And after our all-night fifty-mile sail, it was finally just off our bow.

As we approached from the south, I could see that Bird was a flat, sandy cay, with emerald shallows running up to a palm-lined beach that stretched for its entire length. In the middle, beneath the palm trees, were the twenty-five thatched-roof bungalows of the Bird Island Lodge, the island's only hotel. At the north end were...

"My god," I said. "So that's how the island got its name."

What I had first taken for an early-morning rain cloud were more than a few of the millions of sooty terns that came to breed on the island every year between May and October. And I learned, as we drew closer, that breeding was not a business sooty terns conducted quietly. I wondered how people staying on the island coped with all the noise.

"What noise?" asked the first people I spoke to, a young English couple I came upon unexpectedly as they were passionately communicating with each other on the beach.

The beach was white sand, and the wavelets rolling onto it were about ankle-high, at least for those of us standing. As I might have guessed, the couple were on their honeymoon. In fact, they had been married in the Seychelles. "For political reasons," said the young woman, who appeared well on her way to getting a sand burn as well as sunburn.

"The guest list was becoming impossible," she said. "So, we decided that the farther from home we held the wedding, the more people we could invite without fear of them coming. This was the farthest from home we could get."

They held the wedding at a hotel on Mahe. The wedding party had consisted of the bride and groom, their parents, and a nice couple they'd met on the beach the previous day.

Honeymooners, of course, are not necessarily reliable informants about such things as distracting noise. But the next couple I met, who also happened to be English, couldn't have been more reliable. Or so I assumed by the his-and-hers binoculars they wore around their necks.

I met them at the lodge's bar, where they were having tea "as a refreshment against the heat." The bar, of beautifully polished wood, looked so much like the bow half of a real fishing boat that I wasn't surprised when, later, I was walking out past the airstrip and discovered the sawed-off stern half. The couple began not by introducing themselves but by introducing some of the birds of the Seychelles.

"That one on the teaspoon is a Madagascar fody," said the man. "That one with his head in the breadbasket is a barred ground dove."

"And I believe you are familiar," said the woman, inclining her chin upward, "with the sooty tern."

"Ah yes, the sooty tern," I said. "Does all the noise they make bother you?"

"What noise?" she responded.

George Norah, who managed the Bird Island Lodge, assured me that I wouldn't be on the island long before I, too, would cease to hear the sounds of the terns. He also told me that if it weren't for the lodge, the birds of Bird Island might not be there at all.

Originally, the 170-acre island had been so thick with terns that one of the first written descriptions of it, in 1771, reported "birds innumerable." But over the years, gathering guano, which is a fancy name for bird poop, collecting sooty tern eggs, which Tele told me are considered a local delicacy, and the development of a coconut plantation, which covered the open areas the birds required for nesting, had dramatically reduced the tern population and forced most of the survivors to go elsewhere.

When the most recent owners bought the island in 1967, they started clearing the area at the north end, where the terns traditionally nested.

"In 1967, there was only a very small colony here—about 20,000 pairs," George said. "We've now got, at last count, about three million birds."

Here, it seemed to me, was a rare case of man tinkering with nature in a way that benefited nature.

Another Bird Island resident who seemed to have benefitted from the coming of the lodge was Esmeralda, a 657-pound male land tortoise listed in the *Guinness World Records* book as the world's heaviest of its kind.

The tortoises of the Seychelles are the same species as those in the Galapagos. In fact, they far outnumber their Pacific counterparts. Most live on the isolated atoll of Aldabra, where the population is over 150,000. But a few, such as Esmeralda, had been transported to the more populated islands in the group, where their primary function seemed to be to show up in the photographs of visitors.

"We're celebrating Esmeralda's 200th birthday this year," said George, "but the truth is you don't really determine a tortoise's age. You just guess."

The same went for names. "It is very difficult to determine the sex until they are fairly mature. So, you give them a name, and you have a fifty percent chance of being right," said George.

Or, it seemed to me, you could name them Pat.

* * *

In the morning, we sailed for Praslin, second largest of the granite islands. In a cove not far from where I had the exquisite pleasure of standing alone on the deck of the *King Bamboo* and waving nonchalantly to the entire complement of passengers and crew aboard the cruise ship *Renaissance VIII*, we anchored not far from the Seychelles' most famous attraction, the Vallee de Mai.

As I stood in the leaf-filtered afternoon light, I could see why British General Charles "Chinese" Gordon, who had studied the Bible daily right up until he lost his head, literally, during the defense of Khartoum, in Sudan, in 1885, had concluded after visiting the Vallee de Mai that the Seychelles were the site of the Garden of Eden.

Even though much of the time I spent in the valley was punctuated by the wailing cries of an Italian tourist who had lost the lens cover for his camera, I could see that it was a place of shadows and stillness. A place of towering palms that looked as if they were designed as companion pieces for long-necked dinosaurs. A place of so much tropical greenery that even the most fashion-conscious Adam and Eve would have found plenty to wear.

Never mind that tradition says the forbidden fruit was an apple. In the clothes-optional climate where the Garden of Eden was surely located, a coconut would have been a more likely choice. And no coconut would have been more appropriate than the singularly erotic coco de mer, which grows naturally almost nowhere in the world but the Vallee de Mai. My guide, Therese Lablache, explained to me in a commendably professional manner that the nut of the coco de mer is remarkably similar in size and shape to the female pelvic region—the conformation that has earned it the nickname "love nut."

There was, however, a difficulty with Gordon's theory. The Garden of Eden requires a serpent, but the Seychelles doesn't have any. At least any that could be considered harmful to man.

* * *

If I needed more proof that the Seychelles was paradise, I discovered it the next day when, setting out on my own, I took the morning ferry over to nearby La Digue, famous in some circles as the island where the soft-porn classic *Goodbye Emmanuelle* was filmed.

It wasn't just the slow pace of La Digue that made it a paradise. However, I was delighted to discover, as I hiked along its leafy trails and roads, that most of the vehicles on the island were either bicycles or ox carts. Nor was it just that La Digue was home to the paradise flycatcher, prettiest of the Seychelles' many species of rare birds.

What made La Digue a paradise was that no matter how hard I tried, I couldn't be alone on some of the world's most beautiful beaches because I had to share them with models posing for French fashion magazines or Italian beachwear catalogs.

"Yes, they are here all the time. Terrible, n'est-ce pas?" said a bearded Frenchman whose tone made me suspect his sincerity.

On the beach at Point Source d'Argent, in the shade of a huge granite boulder that looked as if it had been carved by an artist who did not believe in sharp edges, the Frenchman was selling souvenirs. "Good prices on turtle shell jewelry," he said, neglecting to mention that turtle shell jewelry had been banned from import by just about every country in the world.

When I mentioned the ban, he cheerfully admitted he was aware of it and that even in the Seychelles the days of being able to sell turtle shell jewelry were numbered. He said that was why he was rapidly expanding his line of souvenir T-shirts. "This is my best-seller," he said, holding up a shirt that featured a picture of a suggestively posed coco de mer and the words "Love Nut."

I saw two of the shirts on the afternoon ferry back to Praslin and another on the beach while I waited for the *King Bamboo* crew to come pick me up in our dinghy.

That evening, Tele grilled a whole snapper in a sauce of oil, garlic, ginger, chili peppers, tomatoes, and onions. We washed it down with a plastic jug of homemade toddy, the fermented sap of a palm tree. The toddy may or may not have been the reason I finally made some headway in my efforts to pick up a few impolite but useful local expressions from the crew, who sometimes spoke in English, but more often in French, and most often in Creole.

* * *

The next morning, we started for Mahe earlier than a visitor who had just tried his first toddy the previous evening should have to. The crossing was uneventful, though, except that we were overtaken by a plastic sandal that had apparently been lost on the beach at Praslin. And in the harbor at Victoria, we went our separate ways—the *King Bamboo* crew back to Praslin to pick up another charter, me to visit a place I'd been hearing people describe in terms that made it sound more mythical than the Vallee de Mai.

The place was a U.S. satellite tracking station whose dish, protected by what looked like a 100-foot-diameter golf ball, sat atop one of Mahe's highest points. The myth was that the Americans who lived on the site had life made. All their worldly needs were supposedly supplied for next to nothing and shipped in by such means as the huge C5 military cargo plane that had made the island rumble as it lumbered off the runway the day I arrived.

Built in 1963 on a site chosen because the Seychelles is on the opposite side of the globe from a base station in Sunnyvale, California, it had had as many as 300 Americans in residence at one time. But the number was now down to seventy, almost all civilians.

"The Americans are accepted in the community, but because of their duty-free, and everything so cheap to them at their facility, they don't mix much," said a local I shared a Sey-Brew beer with at the Pirate Arms, a Victoria restaurant that is a forum for speculation, intrigue, and gossip.

"What exactly do they do up there?" I asked.

My new friend looked around to see who was sitting near us. Then he leaned close, having the presence of mind as he did so to slide the bill nearer to my side of the table. "They are spies," he said in a low voice. "They are watching the Russian satellites."

* * *

"Watching Russian satellites?" laughed James K. Webb, a friendly-seeming South Carolina native who invited me to visit the tracking station. "We have so many of our own up there that we have our hands full just keeping track of them."

Looking around the nearly deserted bar at the Satellite Club, I noticed something that made me think he was very likely telling the truth. The TV above the bar was showing the same local programming that was all anybody in the Seychelles could get. It seemed that if the Americans had a sophisticated electronic spy network, they at least would have been able to pull in old episodes of *M*A*S*H*.

"We don't live any special life here," said James, who had been in the Seychelles for twenty-five years. "We drink Sey-Brew. We usually don't know what's going on in American sports. And I drive an old car that I need to get into the shop.

"But there's one part of the myth that's true," he added. "The grill at the Satellite Club makes the best cheeseburger in the Indian Ocean."

After a cheeseburger that did seem myth affirming, I headed down the west side of the mountain then along a calm bay where little girls with purple and yellow ribbons in their hair were wading in the shallows. In an area of thick greenery, I came to the home and studio of an artist, Michael Adams, who was himself a Seychelles institution of almost mythical stature.

Although the Seychelles is known for the beauty of the sea surrounding it, Michael had made his reputation by painting tiny patches of Seychelles jungle, mostly on Mahe and in the Vallee de Mai. "I seldom paint the sea," he told me. "I am a forest person."

He was painting the forest in Uganda in 1972 when he decided that Africa had become too violent. Coincidentally, the airport on Mahe had opened just the year before, making the Seychelles accessible to outsiders other than those who arrived on the ships that called once or twice a month. So, he went to the Seychelles on the recommendation of a friend who, he later learned, had never been there.

He liked the tropical lushness he found. It reminded him of Africa's great forests and his native Malaysia, where his father had been an English rubber planter. But it was not the vegetation that kept him. "I'm here," he said "because I like the people."

And it showed in his work. The paintings he did in Africa were landscapes, devoid of people. In much of his Seychelles work, people were the focus.

"I like the way they know how to relax," he said. "To see it, all you have to do is watch them waiting for a bus. They assume many positions, and they are always paintable. I focus on the extremely young and the extremely old, especially the old men. They are an exotic bunch who you never see without their hats on. I think they go to bed with their hats on."

Michael said that when he first arrived, the old men used to put their shoes on only when they arrived at the edge of town. "If my work has a message at all, it is just to take your shoes off and feel the earth again."

From Michael's studio, with a print of one of his watercolors rolled up in a mailing tube in the trunk of my rented car (the print was titled "Bertha Fayette Will Bring Jacques the Key Again"), I headed back past the tracking station and over the spine of mountains. On the way down the other side, I got caught behind a wide, slow-moving truck whose driver seemed to be reading a newspaper. I was about to show him how people from American cities drive, when I came to a scenic overlook, where I could see, out on the ocean, a sailboat heading for Praslin.

I pulled off the road and got out of the car for a better

look. Sure enough, it was the *King Bamboo*, looking as slow as ever. When you are in paradise, I reminded myself, what difference does it make how fast you get from one part of it to another?

   I took off my shoes and felt the earth.

13

Listening to the Greeks

When people ask me to name my favorite place in the world, I often answer "Anywhere I haven't been." But that's a bit disingenuous, and some people keep pressing. So, for a long time, I said New Zealand.

I like the rugged, natural beauty of the South Island. And the waters of the Bay of Islands, on the North Island. And I like the Kiwis, as New Zealanders call themselves.

Typical was a couple I met while they were on holiday in Australia. "If you ever get to Auckland, come stay," they said. And they didn't seem to mind when I called from the Auckland airport four days later, asking if they could put me up.

Not only did they welcome me into their home, but they took another few days off work, showing me all over the North Island, from the hot springs at Rotorua to the wine country around Hawkes Bay. Thanks to them, I know that Hokey Pokey is an ice cream flavor and that, to hear a Kiwi say it, sex comes just before seven.

But New Zealand can be too quiet for my taste. And there are all those sheep jokes. And then I fell in love with the Greek Islands.

* * *

Islands magazine said they wanted me to do a story about an island-hopping adventure but that they'd run too many stories recently on my first choice, the South Pacific. So, I went to

Greece, and since then it has been the country I have returned to more than any other.

* * *

The story began on an autumn day warm enough to signal that we were in the stretch of fine weather the Greeks call the Little summer of St. Demetrius. It began in a taverna in Piraeus, a port so ancient that Plato's *The Republic* begins "I went down to Piraeus yesterday...." And it began with a plan that required me to pick up my bag at the sound of every ferryboat whistle.

The plan was a classic example of what can happen if you leave some travelers alone for too long with a good map. In this case, the map was *Baedeker's Greek Islands,* showing that sixty-two of those islands could be reached by ferryboat. I would get on the first ferry that came along and take it to whatever island it was headed for. Then, I'd get on the next ferry, and the next, and the next, until I'd visited all the islands in the Aegean and Ionian seas or come up against the plan's one major flaw.

While Odysseus convinced his wife that he needed ten years for essentially the same journey as mine, I was on a considerably tighter schedule and had been able to negotiate little more than a month.

My plan was a crazy one, the taverna owner assured me, after first getting me seated in front of an order of calamari and a small glass of ouzo to wash it down with.

"You visit the Greek Islands you need to stay not minutes or hours, but weeks," he said, speaking the English he had learned, among other places, in what he claimed was his favorite American locale, Boston's now long-defunct adult entertainment district once known as the Combat Zone.

I said that normally I would agree with him. My inclination was to linger. And if I could have looked into the future, I could have told him that of all the places I would linger most it would be the Greek Islands. But I couldn't stay this time because, as Odysseus had been before me, I was on an ultimate island-hopping adventure.

* * *

The main Athens port for ferryboats to the islands, Piraeus was almost universally described by guidebooks as dirty and unpleasant. And I suppose it was, especially if you had no particular appreciation for stores whose grimy display windows featured only such items as ship's fire extinguishers, or if you felt uncomfortable buying your newspaper from a corner kiosk that also sold John Wayne *Sands of Iwo Jima* commemorative survival knives.

I, on the other hand, liked Piraeus. And not just because my interest in maritime art led me to its naval museum, whose 13,000 exhibits included what was undoubtedly the world's most extensive collection of paintings depicting Greece's age-old enemy, the Turks, getting the worst of it in sea battles.

I liked the block after block of waterfront ticket agencies, each with a magic-carpet display-board listing island destinations and departure times. I liked the tavernas and the fast-food joints, virtually all filled with young backpackers studying maps and guidebooks and listening intently to such freely offered advice as "You've got to get to Ios. It's the party island."

What I liked best, though, was my hotel, a run-down, side-street accommodation close enough to the harbor so that from my room, I could often hear, over the ever-present din of motorbikes without mufflers, the sound of ferryboat whistles.

* * *

On my first day at the hotel, I came down to the dimly lit lobby late in the afternoon to find two rough-looking men sitting at a table, drinking coffee from tiny cups and arguing animatedly about something. Perhaps to do with the government. Or the economy. Or the American soap opera *The Bold and the Beautiful*, showing with Greek subtitles on the television screen mounted high on the wall opposite them.

Hesitatingly, I approached the men, one of whom had several days of stubble on his chin and the other wearing a dirty gray suit it looked as if he'd fought for, with someone two sizes larger than he was. Their appearance gave me misgivings about speaking with them. But speaking with them was why I had come to Greece. So, I asked myself "What is the worst that could happen?" trying not to think about the veiled women in Egypt who had stoned me.

"Kalimera, hello," I said, realizing a second too late that I'd wished them "Good Morning" when it was four o'clock in the afternoon. In the palm of my right hand, I held, as casually as I could, my tiny tape recorder.

The man with the stubble sipped his coffee, ignoring me. The man in the dirty suit stared hard, at the tape recorder and my face, before demanding, finally, "What you want?"

"I'm . . . I'm an American writer. And I want to . . . listen to Greeks."

During the silence that followed, I had time to remember reading somewhere that the logical end of a travel tale is the return of the hero or his violent death.

The man in the suit spoke again, to his companion. "Is tape machine," he said, pointing at my recorder. "My last year in New York, while I get divorced, I use one. I hide in my underwear."

He leaned toward the recorder. "Hello, America. My name Kostas. I fine. You?" He smiled, not too menacingly, and pulled a chair from under the table. "So anyway, sit," he said. "How you drink you coffee?"

That was the first of more than a hundred conversations I taped during that Greek Islands journey, employment that, above almost anything else I could think of, made me happy.

* * *

I was less happy with my first look at the Greek ferryboats. Modern, sturdy, and hundreds of feet long, very few appeared to be so old or poorly maintained that simply riding on them promised an adventure.

The ferries were a far cry from the vessels that floated through my original imaginings of Greek island hopping. Those had been the rusty steamers that, in reality, were used almost exclusively in foreign commerce and the small wooden caiques, which were once the lifeblood of Greek inter-island travel but were now employed chiefly for fishing and tourist excursions. Yet, I would discover that Greek ferryboats, despite their generally unromantic appearance, did have much to recommend them.

For one thing, ferryboats allowed a traveler to be wonderfully free of the tyranny associated with air transport. Unlike an airplane, a Greek ferryboat always seemed to have room, even if, as was said to happen in the madness of July and August, passengers were crowded into the bow and stern areas usually reserved for the heavy gear and machinery associated with docking and anchoring.

Tickets (whose prices were set by the government) cost about the same no matter when or where you bought them. Back then, you could even buy them on board after departure. This meant that on more than one occasion, I didn't have to commit to going until just before the distance between the ferry landing and the boat's stern ramp became greater than I could jump.

And like most of the essentials of Greek island life—Greek coffee, souvlaki, a room within walking distance of a beach—ferryboat tickets were cheap. So cheap that if you started for one island and, along the way, the boat stopped at another island that suddenly caught your fancy, you could step ashore with no sense of guilt other than—if you'd ripped up your ticket and thrown it to the winds—environmental.

But the greatest advantage of a Greek ferryboat, and one of the reasons I became so enamored with the Greek Islands, was that no other form of transportation seemed more ideal for initiating a conversation. What better opening gambit could there be, as you glided along through a Mediterranean-blue sea, than "Excuse me, but do you know the name of that island?"

It was a line I often used because the constant of a journey aboard a Greek ferryboat is islands.

* * *

Headed for my first Greek island, Sifnos, aboard the ferry *Kimolos*, which could carry 1,300 passengers and 140 vehicles, and in the summer often did, one of the first people I talked with was Second Officer Panagiotis, who invited me into the ship's pilothouse simply because I'd expressed an interest in learning about his vessel and was willing to ignore the sign on the pilothouse door that said "No Admittance."

"The most difficult thing about working on a passenger ferry," Panagiotis told me, "is passengers."

Among the passengers who caused the most problems, he said, were those who had not intended to be passengers. Because tickets were often not collected until after the boat was underway, family and other well-wishers could say their goodbyes aboard before making a hasty jump to the dock. But on occasion, a well-wisher would fail to get off in time and involuntarily become a passenger. Always, they demanded that the boat turn around, and always, it continued on its course.

"They think we are taxi," said Panagiotis. "But we are not."

Most involuntary passengers finally accepted their fate, a fate often made more bearable by the realization that it elevated them, at least in their minds, from one of a journey's well-wishers to one of its heroes.

But Panagiotis remembered one involuntary passenger who did not accept his fate. He was an Athens businessman who'd come aboard in Piraeus to see off his daughter and discovered he'd stayed too long when he noticed the waterfront moving by the boat's rail.

"He say, 'Stop, stop. I jump, I jump,'" said Panagiotis, who recalled that the man, like any businessman in similar circumstances, claimed he had a very important meeting.

"I say, 'You wait. We come back tonight.' But he say, 'No, I jump now.'"

The man, his shoes and briefcase in hand, was climbing over the rail when the crew grabbed him. And they had to hold him until they were far out on the Aegean.

Looking at the Aegean from my vantage point high up in the pilothouse, I tried to imagine what kind of business meeting might drive a man to attempt jumping overboard rather than miss it. But having limited experience with business meetings, my imagination failed me.

Aboard my next ferry, the *Milos Express*, which I took from Sifnos to Folegandros, in the Cyclades, I talked with a Dutch woman who explained, while she rolled what looked like a small cigar, that Greece was a good country for neophyte travelers, even solitary females. The basic honesty of the Greeks, she said, allowed you to make all the neophyte traveler's mistakes without getting into too much trouble.

"But the problem with traveling alone," she added, as we gazed out at the island of Milos, where the famous classical statue of Venus de Milo was found in the early 19th century, "is that Greek islands were made for people in love."

Aboard the ferry after that, the *Rodanthi*, I learned from a schoolteacher who stood next to me while we were waiting to depart from Karpathos that the black-clad ladies on the landing were moaning and flailing their arms because "The man is finished." The explanation became clear enough when a pickup truck bounced up the boat's stern ramp with a coffin in the back.

Aboard the smallish *Nissos Kalimnos*, while watching dolphins play between Simi and Tilos, I talked with a Greek Australian who had visited his parent's Greek birthplace with the thought of moving there himself. But he'd already decided to return to Australia, he said, after witnessing on an Athens street what his cousin described as a typical Greek moment: two men, strangers, each about fifty years old, fist-fighting and head-butting in an argument over a parking space.

As the 2,000-passenger *Superferry* strained against its stern lines at the landing at Tinos, holiest of all Greek islands, I watched one Sunday afternoon from my third-deck vantage point as a vast number of worshipers boarded after a weekend pilgrimage to Tinos from the Athens back-door port of Rafina.

Mostly older women dressed in black, the worshipers seemed to be engaged in a spectator sport similar in some respects to American football, except that the team on offense got to use vehicles.

I could see that so many devout ladies were pressing against a near-to-buckling barricade that the ship's crew were letting them on in groups. When the gate in the barricade opened, the pilgrims—many of them laboring under the weight of shopping bags overflowing with replica icons, plastic holy water bottles, and fire-hydrant size sticks of incense—rushed toward the ferry in a turmoil of pushing and shoving that made me speculate they must be firm in their belief that God helps those who help themselves.

I thought that I alone might be thinking unkind thoughts about the scrambling ladies when a young man standing a few feet down the stern rail from me happened to catch my eye. Nodding at the thick crowd below us, where the half dozen speediest members of a newly released wave appeared as if they were going to reach the stern ramp in a dead heat, he turned to me and started making the sounds of a revving racecar engine. I acknowledged his insight with a smile.

As we rolled from Athens toward Aegina aboard the landing-craft-type ferry *Athaia* on a day that was too rough for the hydrofoil craft to run, a group of schoolboys explained to me that the best thing about U.S. automobiles was their ability to withstand the rigors of high-speed chases.

On a smoky afternoon aboard the *Myrtos*, in the Ionian Sea, I asked a young Greek woman the name of the high green island for which we were headed. She answered "The best island, Cephalonia, where I am from." Apparently, the island wasn't so fine, however, that she was in any hurry to return there permanently from her job in Athens as a gymnastics instructor. "On island, the thinking is old," she said. "In Athens, it is new."

* * *

I did not do all my marveling and conversational adventuring from the rail of a ferryboat. There were also the tables at the tavernas, usually those nearest the ferry landing, where I sipped coffee, or retsina, or ouzo and recorded hour after hour of conversations that might never have ended if I hadn't had boats to catch.

On Folegandros, while sipping a metrio, a half-the-sugar version of the sweet, sludge-like Greek coffee served (thank Zeus for small favors) in tiny cups, I listened for a long time to a hotel owner talk about how the island's lack of sheeps was hurting tourism. You can imagine my relief when it finally dawned on me that he was trying to explain a lack of ships, or ferryboats.

While savoring the licorice taste of ouzo on Crete, I watched a young boy beating an octopus on the harbor seawall. I was fascinated to learn from a waiter that when the boy had tenderized the octopus enough, by whacking it about a hundred times, it would be ready to sell to a taverna, probably the very one I was sitting in. I was even more fascinated to learn, right before deciding to go with just the Greek salad for lunch, that by observing where along the seawall the boy caught the octopus, I could probably have determined the location of a sewage outfall.

On Amorgos, I drank a half bottle of retsina, renowned for having a flavor distinctly similar to that of turpentine, while the bartender told me his troubles. The bartender, whose name was Yannis, the Greek equivalent of John, said he had been trained as a mathematics teacher but was serving drinks because it paid better.

"But this job, I do not love it," he said. "When I am working, I am not Yannis, I am actor."

What did he want to do? Go back to teaching mathematics?

"No, I like to learn the saxophone."

On Ithaca, where I was served the instant coffee that, regardless of brand, is known in Greece as Nescafe, I struck up a conversation with taxi driver Lambros Maroulis. He, in turn, introduced me to an elderly widow who lived next door to his mother. After hearing, through Lambros, the story of the woman's life, which included being abandoned by her father when he went to Australia seeking work in the 1930s, I asked if she would mind telling me how old she was.

"She says she is sixty-seven," Lambros said. "And she says she does not mind telling you at all because she is not looking to get married again."

And there were many stories from Santorini, an island often scorned by people who say it is over-commercialized, but of which I find myself thinking, every time I come into the harbor aboard a ferry in the late-afternoon light, that it is one of the most beautiful islands not only in Greece but all the world.

A favorite Santorini story was from a woman who every backpacker on the island knew as Mama. If somebody didn't have the answer to any question, the suggestion was always "Ask Mama." And always, Mama would know.

I found her place, Mama's, next to a laundry off one of the squares in Fira, Santorini's main village. It was a small, glass-fronted cafe with a sign in the window that said "Cornflakes now available."

As I came through the door, Mama, a short woman in her late forties, was pouring coffee for a young couple who had a well-marked copy of *Let's Go Greece & Turkey* open on a table in front of them.

"Hello, baby. Mama loves you," she said to me, waving me toward an empty chair at a table already occupied by a veteran-looking backpacker focused on the sports section of a *USA Today*.

The young couple, too pale to have been in Greece long, wanted to see Akrotiri, where extensive excavation of Pompeii-like ruins was going on. They were attempting to confirm from Mama that the *Let's Go* information was correct about the days the excavations were open to the public, the admission charge, which bus to take, where it departed from, and how much the bus fare was.

"Drink you coffee, babies," was her answer. "You in Greece now. Everything is taken easy. You like the coffee?"

After I told her I wanted breakfast and to know how she had become so famous among travelers visiting Santorini, she pulled up a chair between the sports page-reading backpacker and me and talked for almost an hour about her life.

Her name was Irene. She had been born in a village on Crete, one of twelve children. "And we was very poor," she said. "My family had eight girls. And if we couldn't get married, they send us all over the world."

Still in her early teens, she'd been shipped to Australia, where she got a job as a maid at the Italian embassy in Canberra.

"I didn't speak English or nothing. And I tried to learn it but said, 'By golly, I'm so stupid I can't understand nothing they say here.'"

It took her some time to realize that the problem was they weren't speaking English at all but Italian.

"Mama," said a female voice from one of the other tables. "Is that my omelet on the counter?"

"Sure, but I'm busy," she said. "Get it your own self."

"OK, Mama."

"The kids, they love me," she said before returning to her narrative, which, when she got to the part about living in America with a fisherman who was lost at sea, even the backpacker put down his paper to listen to.

* * *

And for anyone who thinks adventures in conversation, either at the rail of a ferryboat, or a waterfront taverna, or a restaurant on Santorini where cornflakes are available, are tame compared to travel that might involve actual physical risk—the possibility of a stoning, say—let me share one more story, about two women I met on Andros.

While waiting for a boat, I'd settled in at a taverna for an afternoon frappe, the iced coffee in a tall glass that is the drink of choice in Greece for budget-minded people-watchers because it often tastes so bad you have no trouble keeping it half-finished in front of you for hours on end. Not entirely by accident, the table I chose was near two Greek-speaking women dressed in such low-cut blouses that other women were clicking their tongues in disapproval, and men were walking by on tiptoes.

I won't go into the details of how I eventually ended up at their table. Or what they seemed to do for a living. Or why the one who spoke English, a brunette-turned-redhead named Mirela, put her hand on my knee for what seemed like the entire length of the earth's most recent period of global warming.

But I will admit that when Mirela said both she and the other woman, a brunette-turned-blonde named Elena, had something personal they wanted to ask me, I went on the kind of alert you might typically exercise only at the possibility of something like a stoning.

As Elena watched me intently, and Mirela gave my knee an extra squeeze, and I sweated under the Aegean sun, here's what they asked: "What you think of Bill Clinton?"

Luckily, just then, I heard a ferryboat whistle blow.

14

To the North Pole Without Eating the Dogs

Michael Shnayerson moved on from *Condé Nast Traveler* to *Vanity Fair*, and I was assigned a new editor, Irene Schneider. Sometimes, a new editor doesn't see the world the way you do. Or, worse, they don't get your sense of humor. And you end up falling through the cracks. But with Irene, I was lucky. I tried a joke or two on her, she was mildly amused, and in one of our first conversations, she assigned me a story that would take me to the North Pole aboard a Russian nuclear-powered icebreaker.

 True, despite my good fortune in getting the story, ironing out the details did not go as smoothly as I would have liked. Mainly because Irene made it clear the magazine would not pay for some of the more than $1,000 worth of Arctic survival gear I tried to insist I would need to take with me. Gear that included several canisters of a special spray alleged to be an effective polar bear repellant. But we dealt with all that. And not only did I reach the North Pole, but, in one of the brushes with history a travel writer is sometimes afforded, I believe I became the first person ever to make a phone call from the top of the world and get my own recorded message telling me I was not at home.

 Admittedly, mine was not the most important first in the annals of polar exploration. And our journey, celebrated upon arrival at the Pole with champagne on the ship's bridge, followed by a cookout on the ice and—for some—a quick polar swim, was less arduous than those requiring you to lose at least a toe to frostbite and eat most of the sled dogs to keep from starving.

Still, during the journey, I asked around among the other sixty-eight passengers, many who had enough stamps in their passport to have made Marco Polo envious. And most of them seemed to agree that the North Pole was one of the ultimate travel experiences. "Beyond it, there is only space," said one of the thirty-two Americans aboard, some who had already made a reservation for orbital travel.

For anyone who could afford it ($17,000-plus per person, which, yes, *Condé Nast Traveler* paid on behalf of a photographer and me), traveling to the North Pole was an experience that had been possible since 1991. That's when the last of the Soviets—demonstrating that anything is for rent given a suitably capitalistic point of view—decided to charter out a nuclear-powered icebreaker for passenger service during the few months a year the Murmansk Shipping Company didn't need it to keep Arctic sea-lanes open.

The icebreaker, named the *Yamal*, was chartered by Quark Expeditions, a tour company founded by Australian-born Mike McDowell, former geophysicist, South American backpacker, and Lindblad Explorer expedition leader. Quark's efforts were evidence of just how far the cruise industry was willing to go to accommodate modern-day Marco Polos searching for unique destinations. Ours was Quark's fifth voyage to the Pole and only the fourteenth arrival by a surface vessel. According to one of the *Yamal*'s lecturers, Robert Headland, curator of the Scott Polar Research Institute at Cambridge, our arrival put us among the 3,778 people he calculated had ever stood on the ice at the North Pole.

As judged by one of my fellow passengers—a diamond merchant from Mexico City—that made us a group of very special people. True, we did not face the physical difficulties some polar travelers had, he agreed. "But to make the money to come here is not so easy either."

I knew that the physical difficulties faced by some of those who came before us were almost unimaginable. Robert Peary, who spent much of his life trying to reach the North Pole, claiming he made it in 1909 but probably falling short, wrote, "Sometimes, in opening my mouth to shout an order to the Eskimos, a sudden twinge would cut short my words—my moustache having frozen to my stubble beard."

U.S. Navy Lieutenant George Washington DeLong, whose attempt to reach the pole in 1879 ended in starvation or various other unpleasant forms of death for all but two members of his expedition, left these among the final words in his diary: "Tonight for supper, nothing remains but the dog."

And an astronomer aboard the German arctic exploration vessel *Germania* in 1869, recalling an attack by a polar bear in terms that deserve to stand as a monument to detached reporting, said "The noise frightened the bear, and he trotted off with me, dragging me by the head."

On the other hand, I doubt that any of them could have imagined the hardship of crossing an entire ocean, as I did on my flight from the U.S., in an aircraft whose lavatories were out of order.

* * *

"Expedition to North Pole, lane one; expedition to fishing camp, lane two," said the woman in the olive drab uniform at customs and passport control at the airport in the Russian port of Murmansk, where the *Yamal* awaited us.

From the airport, the North Pole expeditioners rode a bus through a low, rolling landscape of forests, lakes, and flowered meadows—alpine without the altitude. Where the road crossed some of the lakes, we were dazzled by the whiteness of Russians along the shore who had stripped down to shorts and bathing suits to take advantage of the warm summer afternoon. I can't confirm that the warmth was unusual, because an early hardship of the expedition was that the local guide who was riding with us to the ship did not have a microphone, and in the back of the bus, we couldn't hear him or get his attention.

At Murmansk's Atomic Port Facility, the *Yamal* was tied alongside the dock with several other nuclear-powered vessels, identifiable by the atom symbol painted on their sides. It was a massive bulldog of a vessel, with a freshly painted black hull and red superstructure. It would have been sinister looking, which is just what a traveler searching for an ultimate experience would hope for. Except that someone had spoiled the effect by painting across its bow what appeared to be the smiling white teeth of a very happy killer whale.

The *Yamal*'s name, derived from the language of the Nenets, natives of Siberia's Yamal Peninsula, meant "End of the Earth." Launched in 1992, the ship was nearly five hundred feet long and carried a crew of 150, including an Austrian kitchen staff. Which wouldn't have been my choice, considering the number of famous Austrian dishes that I could bring immediately to mind.

As I would learn during a tour of the ship, the *Yamal* had two nuclear reactors that burned about a matchbox-size quantity of uranium isotopes each day. That allowed it to develop 75,000 horsepower and allowed us not to worry about using too much hot water or shutting off the lights when we left the cabin. A much bigger worry was that we were traveling aboard an atomic-powered ship at all. Accidents, as Chernobyl taught the world, do happen. We were told, however, that the reactors were so well protected that a sister ship to the *Yamal* could have rammed it broadside at fourteen knots without causing damage to the reactors. Something I dearly hoped would not be demonstrated.

My cabin, which I shared with American photographer Doug Menuez, who *Condé Nast Traveler* had assigned to the story, was roomy, with a private bathroom and two portholes big enough to make me glad I didn't sleepwalk. From the nameplate on the door, I could tell that the cabin usually belonged to one of the ship's engineering officers, something I would be careful not to mention if I met him at one of the onboard parties our itinerary indicated we would be having.

After dinner, at 11 P.M., according to the ship's clocks, I was standing on a forward deck, still in my shirtsleeves, as we glided silently down fjord-like Kola Bay toward the Barents Sea. The sky was purple and red, and the sun was still reluctant to set.

"Nuclear-powered?" I heard somebody with an Australian accent ask in alarm.

How much, I wondered, did any of us know about the journey we were undertaking?

* * *

By the time we were in Murmansk again, fifteen days after our departure, I would know that the geographic North Pole is a mathematical spot at the top of the world, in the middle of the Arctic Ocean. It is 1,460 miles from Murmansk and 440 miles from the closest point of land, an island at Greenland's northern tip. Usually, ice covers it. But on occasion, it can be in open water. Which meant if Santa Claus lived there, as my nieces and nephews had commissioned me to verify, he was probably a certified scuba diver.

I would know that the constant movement of the ice, the opening and closing of large areas of water between individual floes, and the formation of pressure ridges (similar to the way mountains are formed, except that they were thirty to forty feet high), were what had made the North Pole so challenging to reach before the age of airplanes, submarines, and icebreakers. If you attempted the journey by conventional ship, it might get trapped in the ice and possibly crushed, as happened to DeLong's vessel, the *Jeannette*. If you attempted it by traveling over the ice by foot, dogsled, or, as an American had in 1968, snowmobile, you risked drowning.

I would know, too, that the North Pole is one of the two spots on earth (the other being the South Pole) where all parallels of longitude and all time zones come together. At the North Pole, all directions are south, and the time you set your clocks to is simply a point of view. We passengers aboard the *Yamal* used Norway time, for no other reason than that it meant we ate at different hours than the crew, who were on Moscow time.

I would know that each year, because of how the sun moves across the sky, the North Pole has only one sunrise and one sunset, one day and one night. Which is great for all-night partiers but not so great for insomniacs or for those *Yamal* passengers (and I know Doug and I were not the only ones) who would be three or four days into the expedition before discovering that our cabin portholes had blackout shades.

* * *

At the Pole, we would stop the ship, lower the gangplank, and party on the ice. I would be among the partiers not content simply to jump in and out of the water where the ship made an opening in the ice. Instead, I would undertake an ill-advised rite of passage. Wearing only shorts, I would swim a dozen yards to the ship's side, touch it, and then return to the edge of the ice. In the minute and a half my stunt took, I would feel my body going numb. And by the time I was standing barefoot on the ice again, I would know the sensation of having my toes feel as if they were on fire.

On the way to the Pole and again on the way back, we would visit deep-frozen Arctic islands. Returning to the Russian mainland, we would see native people who herded reindeer, visit an abandoned gulag (where we would discover a skull protruding from a shallow grave), and walk among wildflowers on the tundra.

At the early stage of the expedition, however, I was less concerned with knowing any of that than with the question: "Will I ever feel justified in having purchased, at my own expense, all this long underwear?"

* * *

All the first day, we steamed (or is it nuked?) through open, empty ocean. The sky and sea were a uniform gray, and the air was cooler. But our cabin was so tropically warm that I felt it was a hardship I must report. "Yes, temperature is adjustable," said chief passenger mate Bogdan Javrilchuk when I inquired. "For warm air, close porthole; for cool air, open."

At lunch, I talked with Charles Givens Jr., author of a best-selling financial self-help book, *Wealth Without Risk*. Having visited some 270 countries, territories, or island groups, Givens was still only the third most traveled expeditioner aboard. But goal-oriented person that he was, he said he was working on that.

His goal was to visit all 312 places listed by the Traveler's Century Club, whose members had been to a hundred or more countries. "The North Pole doesn't count, of course, but when I reached the South Pole on January 8th, I said, 'I wonder how many people had ever been to both poles in a single year?'"

Apparently, the number, if all went well, was about to become one.

The day was filled with lifeboat drills, helicopter and inflatable Zodiac boat safety briefings, and our first lecture, by Dr. Mikhail Grosswald, Chief Scientist at the Institute of Geography of the Russian Academy of Sciences. Dr. Grosswald was a charming man and an informative speaker, but his enthusiasm for detail had someone passing around a note that read:

"Mikhail, the ship is on fire. Should we jump overboard?"

"First, I think we must consider early man's relationship with fire."

* * *

In the evening, the captain, Andrej Smirnov, hosted a cocktail party. The captain was a trim, fortyish man with the kind of prematurely gray hair one suspected comes with running a nuclear-powered icebreaker. He spoke to us through an interpreter, a young woman whose career I may have jeopardized by teaching her to say, "Hold your horses."

At Captain Smirnov's side was Captain Boris Sokolov, said to be a mentor to most of the captains in the Russian nuclear fleet. And, until a few days earlier, he had been commander of the first nuclear icebreaker, the *Lenin*, which the Russians had just decommissioned after more than thirty years of service. Captain Sokolov was a bear of a man, with silver hair and a demeanor that suggested he had made up his mind to wait us all (the capitalist world) out.

As the cocktail party progressed, though, Captain Sokolov seemed to become more tolerant of us and eventually invited me (along with chief passenger mate Bogdan) to his cabin for an official interview. It started formally enough, but somewhere along the way, the captain's stern public demeanor disappeared, he proved to have a more extensive command of English than he had admitted to before, and he was telling me stories of the polar bears the crews used to keep as pets.

My favorite story was that when guests were aboard (and guests aboard the *Lenin* had included Cuban Premier Fidel Castro and the first man in space, cosmonaut Yuri Gagarin) the crew thought it very amusing to have those guests go up to the bridge by themselves and find nobody there, except for a polar bear, who was standing at the wheel, steering.

* * *

By the morning of the second day, the temperature was dropping. I still had my porthole open, but when walking on deck, I felt comfortable in the down parka each of us had been issued. And I was beginning to be able to recognize people by the color and design of their wool caps.

Our first ice announced itself through a series of clunks along the hull. The Eskimos are said (erroneously, I later learned) to have more than two hundred names for ice. This, I decided, was end-of-the-picnic ice—similar to the kind of slushy chunks remaining in a picnic cooler after the beer and soft drinks are gone. The chunks ranged in size from picnic coolers to Volkswagens.

We also encountered islands: a low, fog-shrouded group called Franz Joseph Land. Except for the few meteorologists and other scientists at several small Russian observatories, nobody lived on them. But Bob Headland told us they had played an important role in polar exploration, mainly by providing (very tenuous) refuge for early explorers, such as Fridtjof Nansen, who were forced to winter over.

"I can't imagine spending a winter here," said one of the expeditioners after the *Yamal's* two helicopters ferried us ashore to Cape Flora, on Northbrook Island, where we saw the huts and other remains left by several early expeditions.

"I can't imagine spending another hour here," said somebody else, who was concerned that any delay in the return of the helicopters could cause us to be late for afternoon tea.

The fog made Cape Flora an eerie place. But it was beautiful, in its own way, with tiny flowers—arctic poppy, arctic buttercup, and purple saxifrage—growing underfoot in the boggy soil. And what sounded like a million birds were nesting atop cliffs of which we could only see the misty bases. We were told we could wander where we liked but that we must stay inside the perimeter formed by a group of rifle-carrying security men, who were there to protect us from polar bears. "Polar bears can be behaving like Mafia in Moscow," Bogdan warned us.

During a lecture, Brian Gibeson, a marine biologist from the California Academy of Sciences, assured us that polar bears are the single most predatory land mammal on earth, even more than lions and tigers. They will eat anything, including man, as was the case with a meteorologist at one of the observatories we would be visiting. And despite their enormous bulk, they could easily outrun a human.

As a purely academic question, I asked Brian what someone who found himself beyond the perimeter set up by the security men—and not in the company of any person he thought he might be able to outrun—should do if confronted by a polar bear. He said one thing that has worked is to walk away very slowly, dropping articles of clothing as you go. The bear stops to investigate each piece, allowing you to get to safety. "Of course," he said, "you might arrive in danger of freezing to death."

I also asked him about the wisdom of carrying a shotgun.

"That would be useful, too," he said. "If a bear got too close, you could put the gun in your mouth and pull the trigger. Because, with the thickness of his skull, the shot wouldn't do much to slow him down."

When we saw our first polar bears, a mother and two cubs, they were on the ice, and we were on the ship. When they saw us, they took off in a double-time lope, scrambling over hummocks of ice and in and out of pools of water. With the giant smiling teeth of the *Yamal* hot on their tails, they didn't look nearly as frightening as they might otherwise, a thought that caused many of us to voice well-deserved pangs of guilt. Not to worry, we were told. Polar bears are afraid of nothing. Which prompted a question: "Did the polar bears stop to tell you that?"

At dinner that night, I talked with fellow American passenger Caroline Ross, the ship's most traveled person. She had been to 300 of the 312 places on the Traveler's Century Club list and was making her second trip to the North Pole. The other time, she'd gone by airplane and landed on the ice. She had been to Antarctica, too, as had most of the other expeditioners. But she was one of the few who had yet to wear a sweatshirt onboard that announced the fact. Instead, she wore one that celebrated her hometown, Kilgore, Texas.

I asked Caroline to name her favorite place, a question that with most travelers is the same as asking where they've been that the fewest of their acquaintances have also been. "Oh, I like the U.S.," she said.

* * *

After another day of shore excursions, including one to an abandoned observatory and another to a walrus colony, we cleared Franz Joseph Land and were into the thick of the pack ice. It was not the icebergs or the mountains of ice I had imagined. Instead, it was a broad plain of relatively thin ice, six to ten feet thick, crisscrossed with areas of black, open water.

The ship's helmsman tried to stay in the open water, where he could make eighteen knots instead of the five or so he could do through the ice. But when he couldn't go around, he attacked directly, the bow riding up onto the ice and then the entire weight of the ship coming down on it, sending out lighting-like cracks for hundreds of yards ahead and, next to the hull, upending chunks of ice the size of basketball courts.

On the bridge, the ice show was spectacular, but the motion was hardly noticeable. However, in the dining room, four decks down, it was advisable not to overfill your wineglass. And in the lecture hall, two decks lower yet, where glaciologist Charles Swithinbank braced himself against the ceiling in order not to be thrown off his feet, the sound of barely yielding ice against absolutely unyielding steel gave a satisfying authenticity to a lecture titled "The Frozen Sea."

From the bridge, I noticed that the frozen sea was mostly the same color as the sky, a uniform gray. But in the pools of water that speckled its surface and in the upended ice, there was often a blue that looked as if a piece of the sky had been frozen into it on a cloudless day. I asked one of the officers if he hated the ice or loved it. He shrugged his shoulders. "Ice is not woman," he said. "It is nature. We must do our job."

* * *

A handful of us, possibly the ones who had been asking the most annoying questions, were invited for a tour of the *Yamal*'s reactor room. The tour started badly. The chief reactor engineer, speaking through an interpreter, began his remarks only to have them interrupted with "Louder, please" from someone in the back of the room. The translator and the chief conferred, then the translator responded: "The chief asks please no questions until end."

Passing through the *Starship Enterprise*-like control room (I inquired, without success, about who might control cabin heat), we were led into a locker room, where we were given smocks, caps, gloves, and thin rubber boots that slipped over our regular shoes. Each of us had a tiny radiation-measuring device pinned to our smock. Then we went into the reactor room itself, which was hot but quiet. With rods sticking out of the reactor's top and some large metal tanks mounted high on the wall, the room looked more than anything else like the milking room of a modern dairy. Except that you would expect the cows to have two heads.

I started to ask something, but once again, the interpreter told me to hold my questions until later. Which was unfortunate because I desperately needed to know if it was safe to scratch my nose.

Back in the control room, after a sensor scanned us, the chief engineer said we'd been exposed to considerably less radiation than if we'd had an x-ray taken at a doctor's office. In the rest of the ship, he said, the radiation levels were no higher than occur naturally anywhere. More importantly, it seemed to me, he told us he had a healthy year-old son.

* * *

The day we hoped to reach the Pole was a warm one, about thirty-two degrees Fahrenheit, with fog and a few flakes of snow. We were all gathered on the bridge, where trays of champagne glasses stood ready. For more than an hour, among pack ice as thick as we'd seen so far, Captain Smirnov horsed the *Yamal* ever closer to the precise spot that would allow the video screen of our satellite navigation system to tell us we had arrived at ninety degrees north latitude—the North Pole.

"Where is the Pole now?" someone asked, for about the dozenth time.

"If he doesn't find it soon, we'll be drinking flat champagne," someone answered.

And finally, he found it. The top of the world. The spot the Greenland Eskimos during the early days of polar exploration called Tigi Shu, the Big Nail. Glasses were raised, hands shaken, hugs exchanged.

"To me, it's not being here, but all the things it took to get here," said an American who, apparently for tax reasons, lived in the Dominican Republic. "It's almost a reflective point, like New Year's Eve," he said. "Not a time to celebrate the day but contemplate the future."

Another expeditioner, an American photographer named Peter Guttman, came in, brushing snow from his jacket. "Where've you been?" I asked, as casually as I could, fearful, as journalists always are, that he'd discovered some angle I missed.

"I climbed the radar mast," he said. "For just one moment, I wanted to stand above everyone else on the planet."

"Just out of curiosity," I asked him, "which way to the radar mast?"

15
The Bikini Test

Irene Schneider and I seemed to get along well enough. So, when she gave me my next assignment for *Condé Nast Traveler*, exploring an atomic graveyard at the bottom of the Pacific Ocean's Bikini Lagoon, I had to assume that the pattern of stories involving a high risk of radiation exposure was only a coincidence.

Nevertheless, as I touched down on the unpaved airstrip at Bikini Atoll, a string-thin circle of low, flat coral islands that not only inspired the name for the world's most famous bathing suit but was also where the United States conducted much of its post-World War II atomic testing, I was asking myself familiar questions: What am I doing here? Will I forever after glow in the dark?

* * *

For the first time in more than fifty years, Bikini, in the Marshall Islands, in the western part of the Pacific known as Micronesia, had opened itself to visitors whose only qualifications were curiosity and a certain level of scuba diving skill. I was lucky to be among the first to arrive, and I was there to spend a week on the wrecks of warships sunk in the lagoon during the atomic testing. These wrecks served as the only essentially untouched museum, monument, perhaps warning, from the dawn of the nuclear age.

I was undoubtedly there for the adventure, drawn to Bikini because it was exotic and remote and had been forbidden for so long. But if historian James Delgado, who visited in the late 1980s as part of an underwater team from the U.S. National Park Service, was correct, it was also because "The human need to confront the past, even its unpleasant aspects, is ingrained in our culture."

Certainly, I had concerns about the radioactivity. But the scientists studying Bikini the longest said it was safe for me to be there. Time had eliminated most of the radioactive residue, they said, and those traces that remained would be a problem only if I ate food that grew in Bikini's soil and only if I did it over a long period. They said that diving in the lagoon and eating the fish that came out of it were safe. And so was drinking the water, which was either rainwater or put through a purification process.

"You would actually receive less radiological dose living on Bikini for a couple of weeks than you would if you stayed home," said William Robison, of Lawrence Livermore National Laboratory, which, under grants from the US Department of Energy, had been monitoring and studying radiation on Bikini for decades.

Yet, I couldn't help thinking, as I stepped out into the sunlight of a perfect tropical morning, that the reason there was no permanent settlement on this atoll of white sand beaches, coconut-palm islands, and a lagoon that could define the color blue, was that the scientists studying Bikini had been wrong before.

* * *

In 1946, before the first atomic tests, Bikini's 167 residents were persuaded by the US government to temporarily move off their atoll "for the good of mankind and to end all wars." During the first twelve years the former residents were gone,

Bikini was used for twenty-three nuclear detonations, including one, a hydrogen bomb, code-named Bravo, that vaporized three of the atoll's twenty-three islands.

In the late 1960s, almost twenty-five years after the first tests, the survivors and descendants of the original group of Bikinians were finally told their "temporary" exile was over. The U.S. Atomic Energy Commission said "There's virtually no radiation left, and we can find no discernible effect on either plant or animal life." So, the Bikinians began moving back. But in 1975, new tests found "higher levels of radioactivity than originally thought." And in 1978, the returned Bikinians, who it was determined had ingested large amounts of radioactive material, were once more moved off the atoll.

When I arrived, the worldwide population of people of Bikinian heritage numbered about 2,200, including eighty-nine who were still alive from the original 167 refugees. Most of them lived on other Marshallese islands, principally the tiny two-hundred-acre island of Kili, where they said they had never felt they belonged. And for most of them, the possibility of returning to Bikini continued to be a central issue in their life.

"They consider Bikini their gift from God, their one place in the world they can call home," said American Jack Niedenthal, a former Peace Corps volunteer who had married into the community and become the Bikinians' official liaison with the rest of the world.

Now, the scientists said several options existed for cleaning up Bikini to make it safe for the Bikinians to return permanently. The top sixteen inches of soil on the main island—Bikini Island—could be scraped away, getting rid of the radioactive plutonium, americium, strontium, and, most significantly, cesium 137 bound up in it. But the cost and the environmental consequences would be enormous.

"You'd have to knock down 40,000 mature coconut trees and scrape away topsoil that had taken centuries to build up," said William Robison. "And you'd be left with an island that looks like white sand beach from lagoon to ocean."

And there was the not trivial question of what to do with the contaminated soil. One suggestion was to build a causeway with it atop the 5.2-mile reef that connected Bikini Island and Eneu Island, where the airstrip was, causing a skeptic to suggest that at least they wouldn't have to light the causeway at night.

A second option would have been to chemically block the uptake by Bikini's plant life—most importantly coconut palms—of the radioactive elements in the soil. Cesium 137 was the major radiological problem on Bikini, Robison said, because it is chemically similar to potassium, which is needed by all plant life but which soils found on coral islands are deficient in. Mistaking cesium 137 for potassium, the palms drew it out of the soil. Anyone who ate the coconuts ingested the cesium.

"So, we started experimenting by adding potassium to the system," Robison said. "And it worked beyond our wildest dreams. The plants preferred the potassium, reducing the cesium in the edible portion to five percent of the pre-treatment level. It was really very simple and very effective."

But even though the Lawrence Livermore studies, unlike the Atomic Energy Commission studies of earlier decades, had been scrutinized and found to be valid by a world-wide spectrum of scientists, the Bikinians had become so skeptical of science—and scientists—that so far, they had been unwilling to accept the potassium treatments as a solution, arguing that it did not actually remove the radiation from the soil. And as long as the radiation remained, they were hesitant to return.

"Our community moves slowly and with much deliberation, because what we learned from the U.S. government in the early 1970s is that in the nuclear world, you can't afford to make mistakes," said Niedenthal.

The Bikinians indeed moved slowly and deliberately on whether to permit tourism. And one of the reasons they had allowed it, after rejecting other income-generating proposals, such as using the lagoon as a place to dispose of the world's used tires or turning Bikini into a nuclear waste dump site, was that this time they seemed determined to let somebody else be the guinea pigs.

"There are many Bikinians who ask themselves, 'Is it safe for us to be at Bikini?' And I think that as they see more and more other people at their atoll, there will be a certain comfort level amongst them," said Jonathan Weisgall, a Washington, D.C. attorney who had helped the Bikinians win $140 million from the U.S. government, much of it earmarked for cleanup. (Still not enough, some experts said, to restore the atoll to its original condition.)

In other words, it was now the Bikinians who were conducting the tests. And as a visitor who had been reassured by the arguments of science that it was safe for me to be there, I was more than willing to serve as one of their test subjects. How often, after all, can a tourist, or even a travel writer, so nobly justify their presence?

Besides, I was less worried about the radiation—I'd already had all the kids I planned to have (funny, how that worked out), and my hair had begun falling out anyway—than I was about the diving, which promised to be exciting, if somewhat risky.

The excitement of diving Bikini would be in exploring its sunken ghost fleet, ten major warships from the ninety-five target vessels anchored in the lagoon during the tests. Among them were the 880-foot *USS Saratoga*, the only aircraft carrier in the world on which it was possible to dive, and the battleship *Nagato*, once the flagship of the Imperial Japanese Navy, from which Admiral Yamamoto directed the attack on Pearl Harbor.

But the dives were relatively deep, most of them between 145 and 170 feet, which is beyond the recommended depth for divers without special training. Also, live explosives were scattered about on the ships, including bombs and depth charges that I feared someone with my minimal level of special training might accidentally sit on while trying to figure out why his dive companions were frantically backpedaling through the water with their hands clasped over their ears.

While I was there, the Bikinians allowed a maximum of twelve divers a week to visit the atoll. The week I went, in addition to me, there were three other divers—all from Southern California and all very experienced. One, a Los Angeles County deputy sheriff, celebrated his 700th dive on the trip.

Solidly built men in their early thirties with haircuts bordering on military style, they looked as if they might find my relative lack of experience a hindrance. But when I brought it up, one of them said "Don't worry, by the end of the week, you're going to have a lot of experience."

As experienced as my dive companions were, I was interested to learn that they had gone through the same process as mine in deciding whether it was safe for them to be there. Just as I did, they read what they could find on the contamination of Bikini and were reassured enough to come but had arrived with some of the same lingering doubts.

"I know that a lot of scientists have been here. And if they would trust their own personal wellbeing, then so will I," one of them said. "But I will be kind of cautious about breathing any dust, in case whatever is in the soil could get in your lungs."

However, I must confess that as we arrived at Bikini Island, it was hard to imagine having any doubts about wanting to be there. I'm not sure what I expected the island to look like—a gray moonscape of charred, smoking cinders, I suppose. But we arrived at a place that could have, with the removal of a few pieces of rusting heavy equipment, passed for just about anyone's vision of a tropical paradise.

* * *

Bikini, whose name is supposedly derived from the Marshallese words lia kwe, which mean "You are a rainbow," is a flat, crescent-shaped island about three miles long and a few hundred yards wide. It is fringed all the way around by a continuous white-sand beach that looked like it had never seen a footprint—an illusion, I knew, because during preparations for the testing, some 42,000 military personnel, scientists, and journalists had been there. Beyond the beach, the island was a lush, green Garden of Eden. Except, of course, that the forbidden fruit was the coconut.

"Sometimes I am tempted, but I never eat," said Edward Maddison, one of three members of our dive-support crew and only two Bikinians among the dozen or so people who were temporarily living on the atoll.

We unpacked our bags in an air-conditioned, lagoon-side bungalow divided into four rooms, each with a bathroom and shower. The bungalow had a government issue, utilitarian look to it, but the rooms were clean and new. Although they were usually meant to be shared, we each had one to ourselves. Tired from a journey that began in Boston, I immediately fell asleep on my bed until, from the pounding on the door next to mine and a voice calling out, "Open up, it's the police," I correctly surmised it was time for lunch.

Our dining hall, dubbed "Ground Zero," was a big, high-ceilinged room in what was the schoolhouse when the Bikinians attempted to resettle in the '70s. On one wall was a photo of a mushroom-shaped cloud atop a mile-high column of very troubled water rising out of Bikini Lagoon. Taken during the second test, an underwater explosion known as the Baker blast, it had perhaps more than any other single image come to symbolize the nuclear age.

On another wall was a color illustration of several young ladies in bikinis, entirely appropriate considering that the bikini bathing suit was revealed to the world on July 5, 1946, by French fashion designer Louis Reard, four days after the first explosion at Bikini took place. I was not surprised, though, to learn that on the 50th anniversary of the test, *Sports Illustrated* declined a suggestion to do their swimsuit issue there.

Lunch was yellowfin tuna steaks, fresh from a morning's trolling expedition to one of the lagoon's passes. But I was too nervous about the afternoon's dive to eat much. Our first dive would be the shallowest of the week—about a hundred feet down to the *Saratoga*'s deck. I am certified as an advanced open water diver, and I'd gone that deep before. But on our short ride out to the dive site, I still got the jitters, thinking, not for the first time, that maybe writing only about five-star hotel stays wouldn't be such a bad way to make a living.

Once I was in the water, though, and dropping down into the blue, my nervousness disappeared. Using one hand to squeeze my nose to equalize the pressure in my ears and the other to occasionally put short bursts of air into my buoyancy compensating vest to slow my descent, I drifted downward. I passed through the warm, still water, past the *Sara*'s ghostly green, yellow, and brown superstructure, past her still-skyward-pointing guns—their coral-encrusted barrels longer than I was tall—toward her football-field size deck.

The recommended way to descend is feet first. But following the example of the divers that I could see just below me, I tilted forward and swooped downward like a fighter plane, leveling off at the last moment and putting a final burst of air into my buoyancy compensator so that I hovered motionless just above the deck. One of the others gave me the diver's signal that asked if I were OK, then, getting an affirmative response, reached out and shook my hand.

I was awestruck by the massiveness of the *Saratoga*, a ship the Japanese thought they had sunk on seven occasions without ever being able to send her to the bottom. Then, remembering how it got there, sunk by the Baker blast when the hull on its starboard quarter was torn open and its bottom plating ruptured, I was awestruck all over again. It made me wonder if we—the world—were like a bunch of kids playing in the basement with matches, having no idea how close we might be to blowing the roof off of the house.

Back on the surface, I was still contemplating what I had seen. But I was also thinking about the next day's first dive, 170 feet down to the Japanese cruiser *Sakawa*, which was deep enough that if we stayed down more than just a few minutes, we would have to decompress to get back to the surface, a multi-stage process of ascent that recreational divers are not supposed to do.

With that in mind, I didn't protest too much the next day when it was agreed that I would skip the *Sakawa* dive and take the morning off to explore the island.

* * *

With Edward in a rusting land cruiser whose muffler was dragging on the ground, I rode slowly along the unpaved road that circled the island. As we drove, what most struck me was that except for a concrete bunker hidden among the palm trees, there was no visible evidence that on this spot, the universe was once routinely ripped asunder. The seventy-five-foot steel camera towers, the equipment shelters, the thatched-roof "Up and Atom" club built by the Seabees, were all gone, removed as part of the original cleanup that was supposed to make the island livable again.

There was a ghost community of sorts, single-room, single-story concrete houses built for the returning Bikinians. Some of the houses were skeletons, even their corrugated tin roofs gone. But some had been put back into use, as storage areas, a pool room, a video hall, and a tiny store where it was possible to buy toothpaste, cold beer, canned corned beef, and a selection of souvenirs that included what were probably the world's only Frisbees embossed with an illustration of a mushroom-shaped cloud.

Just beyond the houses, on the lagoon side of the road, Edward drove the land cruiser into an overgrown cemetery, where the few remaining headstones were all tilted back at the same angle. They were knocked that way, he said, when a tidal wave from the Baker blast washed over the island. During their occasional visits, Bikinians always spent time weeding the cemetery and placing flowers on the graves, he said. "But the old people, they think the bomb blow the spirits away."

A thirty-five-year-old Bikinian born on Majuro, Edward was trained to dive by the U.S. Department of Energy and had been down into the lagoon far more than any other person. Since 1985, he'd spent much of his time on the island and said that twice-yearly radiological exams had always given him a clean bill of health. He had a wife and five children, who had spent part of the past summer on Bikini, until they had to go back to Majuro for the beginning of the school year.

"When I was first here, I really worry. But after I work with DOE, I know the only way you can take radiation is when you eat and drink lot of coconut," he said. "But most Bikinians, they confused. They always ask me, 'How is Bikini?' And they always say, 'Tell those people they gotta make sure we not go there and have a problem like before.'"

Being away from Bikini was hardest for the old people, he said. "They still talk about the island. And they really like to come here when they die. My grandfather, when he was alive, and his sister, they always ask me, when they die, can I bring? But it is a problem, if they scrape the island."

When we got out of the land cruiser to go for a walk on

the ocean side of the island, where Edward said the narrow band of tidal flats that extended out to the edge of the reef were a haven for lobster, I asked if he'd ever tried to get others to come back.

"I ask some of my Bikini friends, but they say they are afraid."

"Is that the truth?" I asked, picking up a Japanese fishing float and heaving it like a football out into the water. "Or do they just not want to be stuck out here with nothing to do?"

He laughed, almost apologetically. "More important with them now is women," he admitted. "Me, I understand. I need my wife sometime."

He said it was hard being on an atoll that never had more than a population of a dozen or so, most of them temporary workers who were not Bikinian and often not even Marshallese. "Before, I almost quit. But I keep my mind thinking, and I say I gotta do this. I don't like somebody say, 'Who work over there? Not Bikinian? Some other guy? From some other place?' But now is good. You tell your story, you say Bikinian is diving. Bikinian is working for DOE. Not important is me. Important is Bikinian."

* * *

In the afternoon, I dove 137 feet to the deck of the *USS Lamson*, a destroyer that had taken part in the original search for Amelia Earhart. Over the edge of its battered deck, visible another thirty or forty feet below me, was the lagoon floor. I remembered William Robison telling me that radioactive material still existed in the sediment on the bottom. And I'd watched enough late-night TV to know that it is where the monster Godzilla supposedly arose from after being disturbed by all the atomic blasts. So, I imagined it might look like some bubbling witches' brew of primordial ooze, populated by creatures with more heads than they were supposed to have. Instead, it was clean white sand, occasionally dotted with fanlike plants, among which small colorful fish peacefully went about the job of being small colorful fish.

The next day, I got down 151 feet to a submarine, the *USS Apogon*, where I watched Edward go even deeper for a better look at a whale shark apparently asleep in the sand on the lagoon floor. On the way back to the surface, the five of us hung onto the metal decompression bars suspended at ten and twenty feet beneath our boat, where we had to wait for up to twenty minutes at the end of each dive to let the excess nitrogen that can cause the bends escape from our bodies. As we waited, two more sharks approached us. Six feet long, they were curious but not aggressive and eventually glided away.

Shallower, but more interesting, and in some ways more hazardous, was a 129-foot dive into a huge interior compartment of the *Saratoga*, where several single-engine dive-bombers, their wings folded, their tires still inflated, the red firing buttons on their control sticks visible in their cockpits, stood as if ready to be rolled out for action.

Fearing that I was going to over-inflate my buoyancy-compensating device and stick myself like Velcro to the compartment's ceiling, I instead under-inflated it and bounced along the floor, stirring up rust-colored sediment and, to the horror of my dive companions, bracing myself against what I at first failed to recognize as a five-hundred-pound bomb.

And finally, my deepest dive, 160 feet to the enormous sixteen-inch guns suspended just off the bottom of the lagoon on the upside-down *Nagato*. Once the world's largest warship, it was now, as I swam alongside it, host to thousands of tiny silver fish that parted like a beaded curtain as we finned our way among them. The immensity of the *Nagato*, and how that had counted for nothing in the presence of rapidly splitting atoms, again brought to mind words of James Delgado:

"As a member of the first generation to live completely under the nuclear sword…the ships…gave me the first true opportunity to assess my mortality, as well as the world's."

But oddly enough, of all my experiences there, it was not that deepest dive—or any of the dives—that I thought best framed the question that the traumatic history of Bikini could answer.

Our final morning on the island, I got up early and walked alone to the ocean side to watch the sun come up across the reef and to imagine what it would be like if I had it all to myself. And I wondered, as I looked at the beach that had no footprints and the palm trees that were heavy with coconuts, if Bikini, which to outward appearances was almost pristine in its beauty, was a measure of how little we can affect the earth. Or how little we can recognize the damage we have done.

16
In Antarctica, Take Only Photos, and Fuel Hose

I generally try not to one-up other people's travel stories. However, when necessary I will casually mention that I've spent Christmas in Antarctica, handing out presents I made from items I'd found during walks amid a landscape that has been described as earth's last pristine wilderness.

For our cook, Wendy, I'd created a mobile consisting of a padlock, a bent fork, a tin can lid, the base of a light bulb, half a hacksaw blade, and the head of a small ax.

For Andy, who at fifteen was the youngest among us and admitted that science wasn't his favorite subject in school, I'd attempted to kindle a greater interest in the natural world by giving him a clear plastic bag full of the bones of domestic fowl. It was a kit, I told his mother and grandmother, for a model chicken.

To John, an earnest scientist who had declared in his North Carolina drawl that considering the way the world was going, the most meaningful Christmas gift one could give might be condoms, I presented what I claimed was one of my own—a foot-long section of abandoned four-inch-diameter fuel hose capped at one end with duct tape.

There were other gifts, too: a penguin made of corroded welding rod, necklaces strung with Antarctic pearls (a jeweler would have recognized them as a rusted assortment of nuts and washers), and all the parts—including a length of anchor chain—needed to build a 200-pound pocket watch.

Odd gifts, perhaps. But we were an odd group, having paid considerable money (or in my case, having had it paid for me by *Condé Nast Traveler*) to be where we were, when we were, in order to take out somebody else's trash.

Among my half dozen friends who a few days earlier had been strangers, it didn't seem like a bad investment. It allowed us to count ourselves among the few tourists who had lived ashore in Antarctica, instead of briefly visiting it by inflatable Zodiac boats from ships. More importantly, it allowed us to convince ourselves we had an answer to the question many visitors to Antarctica find themselves asking: "Do we really belong here?"

The trash, decades of it, was at a Russian research base called Bellingshausen, named after a Russian explorer who, in 1820, may have been the first human to set eyes on the Antarctic continent. The base was on King George Island, in the South Shetlands, a snow-covered, fog-shrouded archipelago that lies close enough to the Antarctic Peninsula that in a year of heavy ice, you could just about walk to it. We were able to tell ourselves we belonged there because, at the invitation of the Russians, we had come to Bellingshausen to help them clean it up.

* * *

Most of Antarctica—ninety-eight percent is the commonly used figure because that's how much is covered in ice all year round—is indeed still a pristine wilderness. It is the White Continent, frozen, uninhabited, almost lifeless. The Antarctica of temperatures that can drop to minus 128 degrees, winds that can reach two hundred miles per hour, and ice that can accumulate up to three miles in thickness.

Unquestionably one of nature's profoundly beautiful

works, it is the Antarctica of which the polar explorer Robert Falcon Scott, not long before he perished on the ice, said, "Great God! This is an awful place."

But there is another Antarctica, too: The two percent where ninety-eight percent of all activity—biological, scientific, political, and touristic—takes place. It is the coastal fringe and, in particular, the finger-like protrusion of the Antarctic Peninsula that points to the tip of South America, six hundred miles away.

Influenced by the Southern Ocean's moderating effect, this other Antarctica is where, even in winter, average temperatures don't get much below freezing. In summer, it is the Antarctica of rampant life, penguins, tourists, and research bases—dozens of them—where scientists have made significant contributions to understanding our world but have had only limited success in learning how to pick up after themselves.

Over the previous fifty years, virtually all the more than seventy scientific bases built in Antarctica had been guilty to one degree or another of treating the environment in a way a teenager might treat their bedroom.

Science had been much guiltier than tourism of polluting Antarctica, part of the reason being that science had touched Antarctica much more heavily.

We seven volunteers had arrived at Bellingshausen in one of the fifteen ships that accommodated most of the 9,000 tourists visiting Antarctica that season. During the same season, only about 3,000 scientists and their support personnel were in Antarctica. But while tourists measured their stay in hours, scientists measured theirs in months, just as they had for decades. According to one study, the result was that tourism accounted for less than one percent of the total human impact on Antarctica.

Scientific bases, on the other hand, had littered the landscape with such discarded trash as plastic bottles, chicken bones, truck batteries, metal drums containing who knows what, and—as I discovered in a landfill at Bellingshausen—a tracked personnel carrier that I hinted, without effect, would have been very nice with my name on it in front of our two-foot-high plastic Christmas tree.

In all fairness, somebody aboard our ship pointed out that when we went ashore, all we had to remember to bring back was our film canisters, candy bar wrappers, tissue papers, and—if we stepped in any particularly soupy mixes of mud and penguin poop—both of our rubber boots. At least for the first few days of our visit, our shelter, food, and comforts were all housed on the ship. On the other hand, scientists had to bring ashore virtually everything, except water, they would need to survive for months at a time.

And disposal of anything brought to Antarctica is complicated. Because of the low temperatures, nothing, not even a potato peel, degrades quickly. Burning can spread wind-borne pollutants. Burying anything—unacceptable to begin with because of the dangers of soil contamination—practically requires an ice pick. And transporting waste back to the country of origin—retrograding is the technical term—is a very expensive form of return mail.

Unfortunately, for many decades, because of the difficulty of dealing with waste, when the choice came to spending money for science in Antarctica or cleanup in Antarctica, scientists chose science.

"It is only now that scientists are coming around to the idea that they have to be more responsible," said the Scott Polar Research Institute's Bernard Stonehouse, a specialist in polar management and ecology and a veteran of forty-nine summers in Antarctica. Among the things that had made scientists come around, said Stonehouse, who was on the ship with us (and had also been on the Russian nuclear-powered icebreaker *Yamal* when I visited the North Pole), had been the pressure applied to public officials in the home countries of Antarctic tourists, particularly Americans, who could see for themselves that if garbage was scattered everywhere something was wrong.

"It was tourists who started to get the place cleaned up, even long before Greenpeace got into the act," said Stonehouse.

Some bases—Greenpeace called it a modest number—were already starting to clean up. And even Greenpeace said waste management and disposal had come a long way since they first inspected Antarctic bases in 1986. But no matter how great the willingness to make up for past sins, there was, at some bases, another problem: The lack of resources to do anything about it.

* * *

Which is how we came to be at Bellingshausen. We were part of a program instituted by The View Foundation, a non-profit, Canadian-based organization created to allow volunteers to help with community and environmental projects worldwide. We were the first of a series of View Foundation groups that would spend four to five days at Bellingshausen, assisting in cleaning it up.

Initially, we were to be part of a group that would live ashore in tents in a relatively pristine area as part of a project to study the effects of the camp and its inhabitants on the environment. But the project caused such a furor among environmental groups, who called it "a new and alarming departure in Antarctic tourism" and an "enormously dangerous precedent," that View canceled it and offered those who had signed up the chance to take part in the Bellingshausen project instead.

One of the ways I rationalized being there was my curiosity about what it is in humans that compels us to crash parties to which nature apparently had no intention of inviting us. (And, admittedly, the pleasure of visiting the only place where you could travel an entire continent without the need of a passport.)

With us would be a staff of five, including a translator, a cook, an operations manager, an American scientist (John Croom, who was making his first trip to Bellingshausen since he'd wintered there with the Russians in 1970), and the View Foundation director, Carol Devine, who had recently published a book titled *Determination: Tibetan Women and the Struggle for an Independent Tibet*, of which one of our party had the nerve to ask, "What's it about?"

We arrived in Bellingshausen along with thirty-four other tourists, who would be staying ashore only long enough to mail postcards and—on the only continent where one is not needed—insist on having their passport stamped.

We had come ashore from an ice-strengthened former Russian research vessel, the *Akademic Boris Petrov*, which, in our tourism literature, if not reality, had been renamed the *Marine Spirit*. The *Petrov*, whose Russian crew said its duties had once included spying on U.S. submarines, was one of nine Russian ships—all apparently with little else to do—among the fifteen vessels that carried passengers to Antarctica that year.

* * *

In the five days before our arrival, beginning with our departure from the Argentinean port of Ushuaia, we participated in the activities experienced by virtually every tourist going to Antarctica. In the notoriously rough Drake Passage, we got spectacularly seasick. Across the Antarctica Convergence, where warm water suddenly turns cold, we mistook glistening icebergs for fleets of ghost ships. We watched whales slap the frigid water with their flukes. We spied on sleeping seals who drifted by on ice we learned to call bergy bits.

Best of all, on the ice, we walked among penguins by the

thousands, far enough away, we hoped, to maintain the fifteen-foot distance we had been instructed to keep, but close enough to see down-covered chicks break through their shells and take their first puzzled looks at the world.

At glacier-rimmed Paradise Bay, on a day we remembered as Three Landings and a Wedding, we witnessed a marriage ceremony between two passengers, performed in Russian and English by the captain, which the groom, a New York divorce lawyer, assured everyone present was entirely legal. (And the newlyweds, we were informed, had registered at the ship's gift shop.)

But then, as the rest of our shipmates consumed their seasick pills and potions to face the Drake Passage once more, we were left behind on King George Island, with arrangements made for the next ship heading back to stop in and pick us up. One of those shipmates, as he was getting into the Zodiac that would take him out to the *Petrov* in time for afternoon tea, repeated, in the spirit of Robert Scott, "Great God! This is an awful place."

* * *

Scott was talking about the South Pole, which was more than fifteen hundred very white miles from where we stood. But at first glance, his words could have applied to Bellingshausen. Its dozen or so buildings, all looking like mobile homes for prison inmates, were scattered across a landscape of barren rock and patches of snow. Exposed pipe and electrical conduit, much of it seemingly obsolescent, snaked in all directions. Rusting piles of scrap metal and barrels filled with refuge were everywhere. Behind a slight rise, a bulldozer had covered an old garbage dump with a thin layer of earth.

"What a wonderful place to do some Christmas shopping," I said to fellow visitor Jim Osborne, who had been assigned to room with me in the faded green building where we shared sleeping quarters and one gaggingly aromatic bathroom with the Russians.

"Especially," he said, "if you are looking for something toxic."

Enviously, we gazed across at one of the seven other bases on King George—the Chilean's Presidente Frei—whose buildings, all uniformly painted sundown red, looked, from a distance, like a counterpoint to chaos. Not for the first time, I wondered at the effort some of us are willing to make to get to places where we have the potential to be very uncomfortable: the sea, the jungle, the high mountains, the desert, and now this spot about which biologist David Campbell, in his acclaimed book, *The Crystal Desert*, had written "Parts of King George Island are rapidly becoming the urban slum of Antarctica."

Before long, however, Bellingshausen was not an awful place. It was home. We worked on our cleanup projects, chief among them, at the Russian base commander's request, cutting up and bundling for removal by ship hundreds of feet of old hose that had been used to transfer diesel fuel from off-lying vessels to a dozen big onshore storage tanks.

We tagged along with John Croom (assisted was the word we used) as he measured water quality and took samples of bacteria he planned to test to see if they could be used to break down petroleum products that had seeped into the Antarctic soil.

And we had what the brochures described as "cultural exchanges" with the Russians, who I am afraid we left with the impression that "We All Live in a Yellow Submarine" is a traditional North American Christmas carol.

In the little dining hall that the View Foundation staff had dubbed Canada House, we seven Americans celebrated Christmas Day with a window-fogging dinner of turkey, mashed potatoes, gravy, stuffing, and asparagus. It was a Christmas dinner much like any other, except that John Croom gave a lecture on the ozone hole, and, toward the end, the question came up, not for the first time, "Can a group of untrained tourists really make a difference?"

Opinions varied from an enthusiastic "Yes." to "What difference does it make, as long as we feel we are doing what we can?" to "Could you please pass the potatoes?"

In one way, I thought, perhaps like the snowflakes that fall on the white interior of the continent at the rate of only an inch or two a year but over the centuries have built up an ice cap that is miles thick, we had made our small contribution. Our main project, the hose, had been dirty, exhausting work. Yet there it was, bundled up and ready to be shipped out. (And not, I hope, all these years later, still sitting there.)

Perhaps there was another difference we could make, too, with the Russians at Bellingshausen, who did not seem to share entirely our environmental concerns.

Among the Russians, there was a young guy who was not unaware of the world. In fact, he asked if I would pass along a message to anyone of influence I might know in America. It was time, he said, for Julia Roberts to make *Pretty Woman II*. But he had not, I suspected, ever given thought to the damage a misplaced boot could do to the fragile landscape.

On the morning of the day our ship was to come, he accompanied four of us on a walk to the other side of the island. As we trudged across the boggy ground, we tourists followed a zigzag course, trying not to step on fragile patches of moss and clusters of lichen. The Russian, however, plowed straight ahead.

We walked to the far shore, where we watched a colony of elephant seals wallowing at the edge of a foggy sea dotted with small, grounded icebergs. I noticed a white plastic bleach bottle half-buried in the mud near the tide line. It was the only bit of trash on the shore, so I flattened it with my foot and tied it to the outside of my daypack.

"Why do you pick this up?" the Russian asked. "It does not come from us."

In one sense, he was right. Plastic containers and wrappings had yet to make their way into Russian society in the way they had ours. During our time at Bellingshausen, it had been rare to find plastic waste. The bleach bottle had probably been tossed overboard from a ship in who knows what ocean. But in another sense, he was wrong.

"Yes, this does come from us," I said. "All of us."

He didn't say anything else. But on the walk back, I caught him more than once looking at the plastic bottle. Perhaps he was thinking that tourists were as crazy as he'd always imagined. Or perhaps he was thinking, "Yes, all of us."

17

Him? He's Just the Dad

If I have a regret as a travel writer, it is that I did abandon my three older kids when they were growing up. You can say to yourself, from whatever distance, that you love them, and you can believe that saying it is enough. But it is not, which you begin to understand when one of them, for example, starts calling you Uncle Daddy.

When that happened to me, I did the only thing I could think of. I said to all three of mine (the fourth would not be along for some years, when I was in my over-compensating, *Finding Nemo,* stage) "Name anywhere in the world you want to go, just the two of us, and we will."

My younger son, Michael, wanted to go to a major league baseball game in Toronto, the closest place where he could see a favorite player perform. On the round-trip car ride from Boston, we bonded by talking about earned run averages, batting a ball around hotel parking lots, and eating almost nothing but hot dogs.

The trip was great, although one small bit of trouble came from an unexpected source. On the front of my car, I had an Aruba license plate. Meaning it to be a conversation starter, I'd bought it for five dollars while in the Caribbean the previous winter. And I now know I should have removed it before trying to return to the U.S. from Canada.

"Are you fellas from Aruba?" a U.S. border guard asked me, to start the conversation.

"I wish," I said, which was apparently the wrong answer.

We were directed to pull out of line, and a couple of guards went through the car while Michael, wearing a baseball cap and a glove, passed the time by tossing a ball into the air.

"Do they play much baseball in Aruba?" one of the guards asked him.

Knowing as much about geography as any American kid his age, Michael answered "Where?"

An hour later, when we were on the road again, with nothing lost but an hour, Michael's only comment was "Can you believe that guy didn't know Toronto is in the American League?"

* * *

My daughter Tina, who was in college and hardly a child any longer, wanted to go sailing in the British Virgin Islands over Spring Break.

When she and her brothers were younger, I'd taken them—just the four of us—on a weeklong sailing cruise in the Florida Keys. And although they had been disappointed that I would not jump into the water while we were underway so they could practice the man-overboard drills I had taught them, I liked to believe that Tina recognized spending time with her father could be worthwhile. And I hoped that's why she wanted to do it again. Either that, or she had grown wise enough to see that Spring Break on a boat in the Virgin Islands was worth a certain amount of parental proximity.

So, *Sail* magazine arranged a boat for us. (The story would also end up in *Fodor's Guide to the British Virgins*.) And Tina invited two college friends. Caroline, whose participation in a sailing course at the University of Florida the week before she arrived on the boat put me in constant fear that she would ask me to demonstrate some sailor's knot I could no longer remember how to tie; and Missy, who, apparently somewhat dubious about the possibility that details of the cruise might appear in print, and perhaps tipped off in some way by Tina, kept making such statements as, "Don't quote me on this, but has anybody seen my eyeliner?"

Beyond Caroline's week of instruction and Tina's cruise in the Keys, the girls arrived with little sailing experience. But they set about learning how to steer a course, raise sail, handle a dinghy, and wash their hair in a rain squall with nearly as much enthusiasm as they exhibited when getting ready to go ashore in the evenings, where other Spring Breakers were always present.

The only concern, mine, was boys. Such as on one morning when I was sitting alone in the cockpit and two callow youths, who were rowing by not quite as accidentally as they would have liked it to appear, rested on their oars long enough to ask me where we were headed that day.

"Norman Island," I answered pleasantly.

Our actual destination was Trellis Bay, at the other end of the British Virgins from Norman Island. But I'd learned that evasive tactics are sometimes necessary when cruising with college students. I'd learned that if I were truthful to all the boys who took an interest in where we were going to anchor each night, there wouldn't have been any room at the anchorage for us.

The girls caught on to what I was doing, but there were new boys wherever we went, so they didn't seem to mind. Nor did they seem to mind that I was usually around. Or so I gathered when I overheard a new boy ask who I was and one of the girls answer, "Him? He's just the dad."

* * *

The most educational of the three journeys, though, was to Jamaica with my older son, Brendan, who at the time wore his blond hair braided in dreadlocks that reached to his waist. We spent a week in July at a reggae festival known as Sunsplash, held that year at Montego Bay's Bob Marley Performing Center.

The center was an expanse of scraggly grass and hard-packed dirt about two football fields long. It had a stage at one end and was lined the rest of the way around by ramshackle wooden stalls.

The stalls sold jerk chicken, curry goat, rice and peas, health juices, Red Stripe beer, coral jewelry, reggae cassettes, reggae tee shirts, reggae magazines, posters of Rastafarian spiritual leader Haile Selassie, all manner of red, black, green, and gold items celebrating the unity of Africa, and, if you made eye contact for even the briefest of instants, "Ganja, mon?"

During the week, a night would typically begin when the first bands sent a few wake-up chords blasting across the quarter mile that separated the stage from our third-story room at a hotel said to front a lovely stretch of white sand beach. However, I can't be sure because we never saw the beach in the daylight.

From the hotel, where we would wake up every evening at about eight o'clock, we would stroll through the warm night to the performing center and head directly to one of the food stalls. For the equivalent of three or four dollars, we could breakfast on chicken, rice, and peas, a meal we'd eat once or twice more before that night's performance ended, around dawn.

Food in hand, we would wander out onto the field, already liberally sprinkled with a standing, sitting, and lying-down crowd that on some nights would reportedly reach 40,000. Selecting a spot with a view of the stage not blocked by the camera and speaker towers, we'd sit down and patiently wait the thirty seconds or so it would take to be approached by a kid calling out, "Reggae beds."

Reggae beds, also known as box seats, were pieces of cardboard or slit-open rice sacks that served as the standard Sunsplash seating and bedding. They went for anywhere from 20 cents to a dollar, depending on your bargaining skills. So, I always paid a dollar.

By the time we finished our meal, the music would be cranked to such a pulsating volume that it seemed like even our discarded chicken bones were up and dancing. And that's how it went all night—a dozen or more acts, performing for up to an hour each, and everybody up and dancing.

Food vendors. Ganja dealers. Police and soldiers. The kids who collected empty bottles. Stage technicians. Video cameramen. And one amazing fellow, standing for hours on the seat of a parked motorbike, lighting one spliff after another, all up and dancing.

Typical was a family on a blanket next to ours. A couple of young kids were asleep. Mom was feeding a couple more. And dad was up and dancing. Then dad stretched out on the blanket. And mom and the kids were up and dancing. The cycle continued all night, all week.

For me, the highlight was the night we were invited backstage. The concert organizers were trying to use the event to promote summer travel to Jamaica, so as a travel writer, I was able to get backstage passes for both of us.

I didn't know one performer from another. But Brendan knew them all and was in awe. Among the names he spoke with reverence were Junior Reid, Maxi Priest, The Itals, Dennis Brown, and Lucky Dube, the latter two now dead, Brown from drug-related health problems in 1999 and Dube murdered in South Africa in 2007.

But that night, they were just guys relaxing between sets, smoking joints, sipping something from paper cups, joking with each other, and paying no attention to us. Until I caused Brendan to go red-faced with embarrassment by asking Maxi Priest if I could take a photo of my son standing with them.

For a moment, everyone seemed frozen in place. Then Priest smiled and said, "No problem, come on over here, rastaman."

They gathered in a half-circle, draped their arms around

Brendan, and clowned for the camera through an entire roll of film. And when they were done, Priest said to him, "You one lucky mon, have fadah come here with you."

I went out of there feeling high. Or I should say higher, because even a non-smoker such as myself could not spend all night inhaling second-hand smoke from the 40,000 joints that were lit at any given time and not feel the effects.

* * *

And that was not even the most educational part of my Jamaica experience with Brendan.

The following year, he and a friend, Kenya, returned to Jamaica on their own. They'd saved up until they had enough for the airfare to Montego Bay, with about a hundred dollars left between them to last the several weeks they planned to stay.

It was the kind of trip that appealed to me. But as a father, I was dead set against them going. However, as a mostly-absent father, I didn't really have a say. So, they went, and in the first few hours after they arrived, somebody talked them out of eighty of their one hundred dollars. Probably in a transaction that had something to do with pot. But I'm just guessing.

So, they walked Jamaica. Sleeping on the ground at night. Swimming in streams to bathe. Eating where they could. Going up into the mountains, where the marijuana grew. And along the way, especially up in the mountains, they met what sounded to me like some rough characters—the kind whose smiles are scarier than their stares.

When he got back, still having most of the original twenty dollars they didn't lose the first day, I asked Brendan what those rough characters had been like.

"Once we got to know them? Not so bad."

18

My Expense Account Tattoo

Among world travelers, two islands have often been called the most beautiful. They are Tahiti's neighbors, Bora Bora and Moorea. From the air, Bora Bora appears as if heaven and earth have been reversed. My favorite, though, is Moorea, about which James A. Michener once said, "Nothing on Tahiti is so majestic as what faces it across the bay."

Ever since I'd first visited Moorea years earlier, on my sailing voyage with the girlfriend who ended up marrying our captain, I had seen the island's lagoon, peaks, and garden-green interior as almost everything a tropical paradise should be.

But beauty is so often in the eye of the beholder that on a more recent visit, while doing a story for *Condé Nast Traveler*, I asked another American what he thought. The American, Jay Carlisle, was then one of the owners of Moorea's Hotel Bali Hai, where the over-water bungalow—almost the symbol of tourism in French Polynesia—had originated.

Jay was one of French Polynesia's so-called Bali Hai Boys, three Californians who had arrived on Moorea in 1961, opened the Bali Hai (now the Moorea Pearl Resort & Spa), and became legendary for their hospitality and their good times. But what, I asked him, had been the original attraction to Moorea? And was the attraction still there?

"When we were still back in California, I had seen some pictures of a man standing in a canoe. And somebody—maybe they were yacht people—showed me pictures of the Marquesas Islands that were just inspiring. And when I first came to

Moorea, both things were here, too. It was the ultimate South Pacific beauty. And today, they are still here, even the man standing in the canoe."

I knew Jay was right because while wandering the thirty-nine miles of coastal road that circles the island, I'd often seen him myself. Sometimes he would be young and tautly muscled, sometimes older and proof that French Polynesia is as fertile ground for weight loss program franchises as it once was for missionaries. Always, though, the man would look as if he had been doing whatever he was doing—even if it was listening to music through headphones—for a thousand years. And once, on the sparsely populated back side of Moorea, near the village of Haapiti, I had even seen—her.

She was dressed in a red and white wrap-around pareau, sitting by herself in a canoe pulled up on the shore and strumming a ukulele. I wanted to stop and talk with her. But wanting even more not to alter the scene in any way, I drove slowly on, smiling to myself with the thought that I'd locked the perfect image of paradise into my head forever.

It was an image, I knew, that painter Aad van der Heyde, who had a gallery in Cook's Bay, would appreciate. Born in the Netherlands, Aad had been on his way to Australia in 1956 when he stepped off the ship in Tahiti and immediately fell in love with French Polynesia. Could he remember, I asked, what had first attracted him?

"When you are twenty-two, and single, and male? It is not the majestic beauty of the mountains and the cloud formations," he said. "You don't give a damn about that when you are twenty-two. It is the women. It is this long hair, this velvet type of skin, this fragrance, like salted bananas."

Wiping the tiniest bead of sweat from my forehead, I said his landscape paintings were lovely, too.

* * *

In search of landscapes painted on a broader canvas, I would sometimes wander, by car or on foot, through Moorea's silent, Eden-like interior, a kind of bowl or natural stadium brooded over by eight encircling peaks. In the days before contact with Europeans, the interior was home to thousands of Mooreans but was now so deserted, except for the ruins of hundreds of stone maraes, or worship sites, that you could almost hear the footsteps of the ancients.

One day, I drove up into the interior with a Moorean named Alex Haamatearii to a promontory known as the Belvedere Lookout, which film buffs might recognize from the Anthony Hopkins/Mel Gibson version of the *Bounty* mutiny.

To understand Moorea, Alex said, all I had to do was look out across the lush interior to the twin glimmers of Opunohu and Cook's Bays.

"Everywhere you are looking at the island is beauty," he said.

Far below, in Cook's Bay, we could see the sailing cruise ship *Club Med 2* swinging at anchor. From our vantage point, it looked like a white feather on the water.

"We Polynesians were very great navigators," said Alex, who seemed to be contemplating the ship. "Because we knew how to navigate using the pig."

Usually, the ancients navigated with the stars, the wind, and the currents, Alex said. But when they got lost, they relied on the pig. "You take pig and put in the water, and the pig always swim toward land. Because the pig, he smell the land more than the man does."

Which gave me so much respect for that often-maligned beast that I vowed to forgo pork at a Polynesian feast I planned to attend that evening at the Tiki Theatre Village, a kind of living cultural museum at the north end of the island, where actor Dustin Hoffman had recently been "remarried" in a traditional Tahitian wedding ceremony.

At the village, in addition to pork, which I compromised on and had only a tiny bite of, you could get breadfruit, taro, and yams. You could get poisson cru, the Polynesian national dish of raw fish marinated in lemon juice, then doused with coconut milk. ("They use coconut milk with everything," a Belgian woman who lived on Moorea said to me, wrinkling her nose as she spoke. "Food, coffee, even when they make love.") And, I discovered you could get a tattoo.

* * *

I'd made the mistake of wandering over to the hut of one of the tattoo artists, a man named Vatea, who was applying, on the shoulder of an ear-ringed young Australian man, what looked to me like a turtle jumping over the moon.

Vatea used an electric needle whose batteries, Duracell alkaline, he had to change in the middle of the process. But the real traditionalists still did it the old way, he told me, with shark's teeth and a mallet. Up to ten people would be involved in the procedure, he said, several whose only purpose was to sing or chant. Very loudly, I assumed.

I asked the Australian if it hurt. Teeth clenched, he shook his head no. "Man never say hurt," Vatea volunteered.

I was not interested in a tattoo myself, I told him, but just wanted to learn a little more about it.

"No problem," Vatea said, with a casualness that should have made me suspicious.

The tattoo originated in Polynesia and was brought to the Western world by sailors returning from voyages of discovery. The Polynesian practice of it nearly died at one time because of pressure from disapproving missionaries. But the Polynesians had revived it a few years back as they took a greater interest in their cultural heritage. The designs I kept flipping back to in his book—simple geometric patterns—were from the Marquesas Islands, Vatea told me, and I wished he hadn't.

For me, the Marquesas had been a romantic icon ever since I read, as a boy, about a young sailor named Herman Melville, who deserted ship in the Marquesas and lived in a cannibal valley with a Polynesian maiden who happily used her only article of clothing as a sail.

And that, I am afraid, did it. I asked a few more questions that I told myself were purely in the interest of getting the story. How long would it take? (Less than an hour.) How much did it cost? (About fifty American dollars.) Did he give discounts to anyone who drew a crowd? (Would any celebrities be in the crowd?) But I was soon sitting on a straw mat, having commissioned a geometrically patterned band to go around my right ankle.

At least no one could say I had done it because I was young and stupid, I thought. And it helped to rationalize, too, that the fifty dollars I was about to spend could be entered on my expense report as "Research, other."

Vatea assured me he used disposable needles and that if I later regretted my decision, I could always—wear socks.

To keep my mind off the less than pleasurable sensation of the hundreds of needle pricks, I asked Vatea if he could explain Moorea's beauty. But I don't think he understood the question, either because his English wasn't up to it, or, as I like to imagine, because he was concentrating on his work and didn't hear me.

"Pain is only a little," he finally said, finishing off the job by smearing my ankle with an antiseptic ointment and then wrapping it in a bandage. "Beauty is always."

It was not an unpleasant thought. For the rest of my life, at least when I wasn't wearing socks, I would have a permanent reminder—very permanent—of the beauty of Polynesia.

19

Turtles for Ancestors

Not long after I got my tattoo, I visited the Marquesas, for *Islands* magazine, where an artist on the island of Nuku Hiva assured me that the geometric design around my ankle was Marquesan. He assured me, too, that he knew what it meant. "It says your ancestors were turtles."

I could be happy with that. In Polynesian mythology, the turtle is a figure of respect. It is a god, in fact. But the trouble was that this artist, whose father did stone carvings using power tools, was one of several supposedly knowledgeable locals who would explain to me the meaning of my tattoo—each giving a different interpretation.

"You are a dangerous man, a warrior," one would say, obviously unaware of my undistinguished record regarding physical confrontation.

"Where crowds gather, you go," would say another, who, I couldn't help thinking with some cynicism, already knew I was a journalist.

"Hmmm," yet another would consider. "I think the man who makes this does not finish."

The reason for these various interpretations was understandable. Many people consider the Marquesas—a dozen major islands, all dramatically high and green, about 800 miles northeast of Tahiti—to rank with Tahiti and Bora Bora among the world's most beautiful islands. But they also have one of the most tragic histories.

During a few decades in the 1800s, the population, once

estimated at as much as 80,000, plummeted to a couple of thousand, mainly because of diseases introduced by Westerners. For the few Marquesans who survived, their culture, history, art, and language were so nearly eradicated by missionaries and other Western influences that they lost almost all their collective memory.

No one could tell me the meaning of symbols as pervasive in Marquesan society as the cross is in Western culture because no one knew.

Yet, despite the Marquesas' tale of tragedy, I would discover, too, a story of hope. It is a story of people who were not only rediscovering their past—often with so little historical evidence to guide them that what they were doing was re-inventing themselves—but who were also leading a cultural revival spreading throughout French Polynesia.

"They know they must live in the future," Patrick Chastel, a French schoolteacher on the island of Hiva Oa, told me. "But they have also learned, because of the big hole in their history, that if they are not to lose their self, then they must have a past, too."

As any number of Marquesans wanted to make sure I understood, they have a past perhaps 800 years older than the Tahitians, who often dismiss the Marquesans as country-bumpkin cousins, but who, it turns out, are descendants of the Marquesan voyagers who probably first populated Tahiti.

"Tahiti people are Marquesas people, except they don't respect so much the old ways," a Marquesan on Ua Pou told me in an island shop, as he bought batteries for his Walkman.

* * *

The Marquesas themselves were settled from Tonga or Samoa at least by A.D. 500, about a thousand years before they were chanced upon by the first Europeans—Spanish explorers sailing from Peru in search of a great continent rumored to lie at the bottom of the world.

This first Western contact did not immediately prompt a wave of tourism. The next Europeans, who sailed with Capt. James Cook, did not arrive for another 200 years. However, many other ships soon followed Cook's and introduced all manner of novelties to the Marquesans. Including smallpox, which wiped out much of the population. The missionaries arrived, too, the Catholics ultimately proving to be the most successful in converting the few Marquesans who had not succumbed to disease. In the process, they nearly destroyed all the old "superstitions"—communicated mainly through song, dance, and the art of tattooing—that served as a repository for Marquesan culture.

Yet while Western contact with the Marquesas proved devastating (even today, its population is only about 8,000, and many once-crowded valleys remain hauntingly empty), it also helped create, for Westerners, the vision of the South Seas as a paradise. Herman Melville contributed to the myth with a highly successful book, *Typee*, based on his brief stay among the Marquesans when he, as a young sailor, sought refuge with them after deserting his ship and purportedly losing his heart, almost literally, to a cannibal princess.

Another contributor was the painter Paul Gauguin, who said of Hiva Oa not long before he died there in 1903, "Poetry emerges here of its own accord, and it can be evoked simply by allowing oneself to dream while painting."

Intrigued by the descriptions, my dream of visiting the Marquesas had been nearly lifelong. I thought I would see it in 1983, as we had planned to put in there while I was sailing aboard the yacht across the Pacific with my all-too-fickle girlfriend. But thwarted by uncooperative winds, we ended up in the more southerly Tuamotus and, eventually, Tahiti.

What finally brought me to the Marquesas was my desire to discover the meaning of my tattoo, which the artist on Moorea who had done the work had been unable or, it belatedly occurred to me, unwilling, to explain.

I wanted to reassure myself that the artist, belonging to a people known for their love of a good practical joke, had not permanently marked me with a message that said something like, "This is a man who can be talked into anything."

* * *

How great a sense of humor the Marquesans have, and how distinct it is from the Western world's, was made dramatically clear to me during my flight from Tahiti to Nuku Hiva, largest of the Marquesas, aboard a prop-driven plane in which the cockpit was visible from the passenger cabin. We were just finishing the airline-provided lunch—which had come in a clear plastic bag—when a big, roundish Marquesan sitting in the front row blew up his bag and popped it with a loud bang just behind the pilot's head.

The Marquesans aboard the flight (who, except for me, were the only passengers) seemed to think this was enormously funny. But the pilot, who appeared to be French, did not. He involuntarily lurched forward at the sound, putting the plane into a nosedive.

Oh my God, I thought, as we plunged toward the deep blue ocean, it is possible to die laughing.

The pilot, though, recovered in time to avoid disaster, and a short time later, with my heart rate almost back to normal, we descended more reasonably toward Nuku Hiva.

* * *

As with all the Marquesas, because they are so young geologically, Nuka Hiva is mostly a sharp-edged volcanic mountain, with few protecting reefs, no tranquil lagoons, and—of more immediate concern to me—not much flat land on which to have a runway.

The precipitous topography dictated the tiny airstrip's location on the opposite side of the island from the main town, Taiohae, population 1,600, where I had reservations at an inn. I didn't give much thought to what that might mean until I called the inn's owner, Rose Corser, an American who was the only long-time English-speaking resident of the islands I would meet during my journey, and asked how I was supposed to get there.

"There's a road, but we've had some rain, for about three months, so you'll want to take a helicopter," said Rose, a recent widow who, with her late husband, had arrived in the Marquesas by sailboat some twenty years earlier. To cover eleven miles, a helicopter seemed an extravagance. But I followed Rose's advice and—with my heart rate elevated once more—got a seven-minute education in why the Marquesas had remained so undeveloped and why some of the old ways had been able to survive, if only barely.

Ascending noisily from the airstrip and dodging a rain squall, the helicopter rode up and over one of the greenest and most rugged landscapes imaginable. Spine-backed ridges and deep-cut valleys awash with streams and waterfalls made it likely that neighboring communities had often been accessible only by sea, if at all, for most of their history. It seemed a landscape that—smallpox and religion aside—did not easily yield to intrusion. A landscape that could hold onto things. Including, it occurred to me, as we just cleared jagged Mount Tekao, downed helicopters.

Descending toward Tahioe Bay, where the seas rolled in with enough force to make the handful of yachts riding at anchor look very uncomfortable, we clattered down to a landing pad along the water's edge. While waiting for Rose to come get me in her four-wheel-drive pickup, I came upon the first of many Marquesans whose full-body canvas of tattoos would leave me feeling—unfinished.

* * *

Tattooing, one of the few Pacific Island arts to have impacted the rest of the world, was first observed by Europeans when the Spaniard Alvaro de Mendana stopped in the Marquesas in 1595. Originally limited to royalty, tattoos later became a way not only of identifying where a person was from but of commemorating their significant life events. Yet, when I had first visited Tahiti, some twenty years earlier, tattooing had been so nearly eliminated by church disapproval that the few examples I saw were mostly of the American jailhouse variety—eagles, snakes, hearts. In fact, it was usually assumed that someone with a tattoo had been in jail.

More recently, though, all that had changed. Suddenly, tattoos were much more in evidence in French Polynesia, on both men and women. And they were much more traditional appearing. Most were seemingly abstract designs that, upon closer look, might be recognized as human or animal figures, faces, or eyes. Like the best of the wood and stone carvings, the best designs, I was told, were from the Marquesas.

The Marquesan at the helicopter pad was a work of art, too. Although, as I would discover, not a particularly rare one. Not only were his arms, legs, and shirtless chest and back covered in a myriad of designs, but so were parts of his neck and face. He didn't understand English. (Few Marquesans do, speaking first a Polynesian dialect distinct from Tahitian, then French, which they learn in school.) But he apparently took my interest in his tattoos as an indication that I wanted to add to my own—which, compared to his, seemed an almost paint-by-numbers-effort.

I definitely did not want any more, feeling that even in some of New York or L.A.'s trendier nightclubs, a tattooed forehead, say, would have been looked upon with disapproval. So, I was relieved when Rose arrived.

"Oh sure, a lot of visitors get tattoos," she told me as we bounced along toward her waterside bungalows at the western edge of the village. "And most Marquesans think that's fine. They think it shows you appreciate Marquesan culture."

However, a guide I talked to named Jean-Pierre did not think it was fine. Quiet but not afraid to speak his mind, Jean Pierre, who had grown up in a remote valley where Melville once stayed, believed that tattoos should have special meaning. But too often now, he said, they had no other purpose than decoration. It was particularly wrong, he thought, for visitors to get them.

"You don't give a tattoo to a pig, a cat, or a dog that walks by," he told me. "Why give to a tourist?"

A good question—and one I hoped to find an answer for on the next island I visited.

* * *

Ua Pou, the youngest of the Marquesas, was even more precipitous than Nuku Hiva, with a craggy profile that reminded me of Bora Bora and a sloping airstrip with a hook at the end that would make it a delight for anyone who thinks conventional landings are much too mundane.

The six-mile ride to the town, Hakahau, was easy enough, though, and I was soon installed as the only guest (in fact, I was the only guest everywhere I stayed in the Marquesas) at a four-room pension sitting on the side of a hill overlooking a tiny harbor.

The pension was owned by Helene Kautai and her husband, known to all as Doudou (Sweetie). Although Helene herself was Marquesan, she was appalled at my mangling of the French language. At meals, she would often refuse to pass a dish until she was satisfied with my pronunciation of it. In my defense, it is not often one gets to practice the French for "More goat, please." However, she did help arrange a meeting for me with a schoolteacher, Toti Teikiehuupoko, president of the Motu Haka Association, a group founded to preserve Marquesan culture.

* * *

Toti told me the group was formed in 1978 to see that the Marquesan language was taught in the schools, which up until then had held all classes in French. And preserving the language was still the main mission.

"We believe the language is the bank, the reserve, of the Marquesan culture," he said. "We believe as long as the language is alive, the culture will follow."

In the beginning, the church, still a powerful force in the Marquesas, opposed any efforts at cultural revival. The idea that Marquesans could respect God and respect Marquesan traditions, too, was one it had tried to discourage since its very arrival. But the instrument of change, the instrument without which a Marquesan cultural revival might never have happened, sprang, ironically enough, Toti said, from within the church itself.

It came in the form of an enlightened Catholic priest who lived on Ua Pou for many years and whose many accomplishments included translating the Bible into Marquesan. He convinced others that the islanders could praise God through traditional songs, dances, and other cultural expressions. The priest's support of the Motu Haka Association allowed it— and a cultural renaissance that reverberated throughout French Polynesia—to flower.

The association eventually became involved in promoting and preserving not only the Marquesan language but all aspects of Marquesan culture. So, it did not surprise me, when I started questioning him about the cultural significance of tattoos, that Toti, a well-preserved middle-aged man with a professorial demeanor, unselfconsciously slipped off his shirt to show me his own substantial collection.

"It is important to be of the world," he said, pointing out various sections of a life-long work in progress, "but it is important first to be of the Marquesas."

As for visitors getting tattoos, he said he saw nothing wrong with that, if they thought carefully before choosing a design and knew its significance. Mine, he said, represented either the tail of a fish or meant that before I was a person, I had been a mountain.

* * *

Mountains, a spine of them running down the middle, formed a spectacular part of Hiva Oa, of which Robert Louis Stevenson once said, "I thought it the loveliest, and by far the most ominous, spot on earth."

Ominous because of the thousands of pae pae, or stone platforms, once used for house foundations, that still lay abandoned among the lush tropical underbrush. Ominous, too, because the island had a reputation for being less friendly toward outsiders than Nuku Hiva or Ua Pou. (At least that's what the residents of those islands told me.) But for me, Hiva Oa turned out to be anything but unfriendly.

Much of that was thanks to my pension's hosts, Gabriel and Felicienne Heitaa, with whom I spent evenings critiquing the American soap opera *The Bold and the Beautiful* (its title rendered in French as *Love, Glory, and Beauty*). And to Patrick Chastel, who invited me to visit his classroom, where his teenage scholars—after what I thought was a stirring, if somewhat abbreviated, lecture by me on the geography, history, and future of the island of America—wanted only to know how old I was, if I were married, and if I were personally acquainted with Leonardo DiCaprio.

Frustratingly, I could not convince the Heitaas that the soaps (which portrayed an America in which nobody worked and everybody had a lot of money, a beautiful house, and a big car) were not an accurate picture. They, it turned out, had been to America, to Los Angeles. They had visited Disneyland, toured Universal Studios, and spent as much time as possible at what much of the rest of the world apparently considers America's most significant cultural achievement—the shopping malls. As a result, they had seen with their own eyes that the soaps had gotten it exactly right.

"It is finished, the Marquesas Islands alone in the Pacific," Patrick explained to me in defense of the Heitaas' point of view. "But you must remember that while in Europe there was 2,000 years between the beginning of history and now, in the Marquesas, there are only 200 years between the Stone Age and *Love, Glory, and Beauty.*"

* * *

How short the distance is between the past and the present was made clear to me one day when I heard that a German tourist from a small cruise ship had disappeared during an excursion to Fatu Hiva, least developed of the major islands, and that the vessel had finally sailed away without finding any trace of him.

A widespread explanation was that an eel living in a river near where the German had last been seen had eaten him. Apparently, a fisherman had wrongfully killed the river's original eel some generations back. And the feeling was that one of its offspring was just settling an old score. The most hotly debated point was not whether the story was true. Few seemed to doubt it. The big question was whether this was a good or bad use of tourists.

It was a question on which I did not take sides. But the distance between the past and present, and how perilous negotiating it can be, was something I thought about every time I considered my tattoo. Of course, I told myself, I didn't believe in those Marquesan "superstitions." But if I did, what would a background check of my ancestry turn up? A turtle, a fish, or a mountain?

Perhaps the uncertainty meant I could choose whichever interpretation I wanted. Or that, in some weird way, the tattoo artist and the men who interpreted his work understood, as I did not, that I was supposed to choose them all. I have always been drawn to the sea and high places. So, what more appropriate links to the past for me than a turtle, a fish, and a mountain? And who is a more dangerous person than a writer? Are not writers warriors? I know that all my writer friends think so.

And it occurred to me, finally, that perhaps the most telling interpretation was that the man who made my tattoo had not finished it. Because are not we all works in progress?

20

Favorite Near-death Experiences

Despite speculation by the Marquesans that my tattoo might mark me as a warrior, I am anything but fearless. To frighten me, you need only extend an invitation to speak in front of an audience of library patrons. Or Cub Scouts. On the other hand, I am often willing, as I think so many travel writers are, to let the possibility of a good story overcome any concern about dire consequences.

It certainly seemed so when, for *Aqua* magazine, photographer Darrell Jones and I visited New Britain, an island off the coast of Papua New Guinea.

We were in a pair of small outrigger canoes, moving tentatively toward a beach at the base of a volcano whose last major eruption, in 1994, had covered much of the port town of Rabaul with foot upon foot of thick gray ash.

In one canoe, paddled by a local villager, Darrell was snapping away at a thick column of smoke the volcano was pumping into the sky. I was in the other canoe, with my attention focused not on the volcano but on my paddler, the villager's niece, who, every few strokes, stopped to let her fingers drag in the water.

The niece, I realized (and wished I hadn't), was using her fingers to test the water's temperature, on the lookout for any sudden heating that might presage another eruption. And she seemed none too happy with what the water was telling her.

"I'm beginning to think," I called over to Darrell, "that going for eggs wasn't such a good idea."

Earlier, the villager had explained to us, in a mix of English and Pidgin that is the lingua franca of Papua New Guinea, that a big-footed bird known as a megapode lived at the foot of the volcano and used the underground heat to incubate its eggs. But before the eggs could hatch, the locals would gather them, which was a risky business because it required digging down as much as six feet into the unstable ground. Sometimes, the holes caved in, burying the diggers alive.

But as we approached the beach, the villager said nothing—except whatever he was mumbling, uneasily, to himself. A chemical reaction had turned the water near the shore a shade of red that looked uncomfortably like the color of blood. And when Darrell and I jumped onto the beach, which consisted of crunchy, powdery rock, I felt intense heat through the soles of my shoes.

"What a strange place," Darrell said to me, his camera, as always, up to his face. "Would you mind standing over by that smoke?"

Wisely, you could argue, the niece refused to get out of the canoe. But the villager—perhaps feeling responsible for our well-being, or maybe because we hadn't paid him yet—reluctantly followed us up onto the beach. The air smelled of sulfur, and, above us, steam vented from cracks in the volcano's cone.

"When, exactly, did the volcano last erupt?" I asked the villager, becoming more concerned by his nervousness and less sure about my assumption that he would not place us in mortal danger simply for the equivalent of the five dollars we had agreed to pay him.

"Last night," he answered.

Last night, we were having dinner in the village at a Chinese restaurant appropriately named, based on the cinders piled up all around it, the Phoenix, when we heard what we thought was thunder. Now, our jokes about how the restaurant might have to rise again from the ashes didn't seem nearly as funny as they had at the time.

Nor did it seem that we could find ourselves at any greater risk than we currently were. But that's because I could not foresee what would happen a few days later, when, the eruption having fizzled out, we were back on mainland Papua New Guinea and up in the Southern Highlands.

* * *

The Southern Highlands is a relatively small area but so ruggedly isolating that the people who live there speak some 740 distinct languages. Perhaps because of the differences the languages suggest, the Southern Highlanders are noted for their violence. Frequent clan warfare has always been part of the Southern Highlands culture, as has the concept of payback, a system of harsh retribution for every perceived offense, from killing an opposing clansman in battle to accidentally running over somebody's pig with a rental car.

Usually, unless they are in the rental car that runs over the pig, travelers in the Highlands don't have to worry about the violence. The Western-run Highlands lodges generously compensate surrounding villages so that tourists can, without fear, visit, take photographs, and generally act in ways that would make them recognizable as tourists anywhere. And the Highlanders, who are evidence that financial savvy has nothing to do with whether you wear a bow tie around your neck or a bone through your nose, have no interest in killing the Golden Fleece. However, there are times when tourists can do something foolish, as Darrell and I discovered.

We had hired a van and an English-speaking Papua New Guinean driver and were visiting a village populated by the Highlands' most famous clan, the Huli, whose men wear big, mushroom-shaped wigs of human hair. About half a dozen of the "wig men," as they are called, were decked out in their full regalia: bows and arrows, grass loincloths, kina shell necklaces (after which Papua New Guinean money is named), long quills through their noses, and wigs topped with brilliantly colored feathers. As we watched, they painted their faces in red and yellow patterns. They were gracious, if solemn. And they seemed willing enough to comply, for a fee, when I suggested that it would be interesting to have our faces painted just like theirs.

With the painting completed, we learned that the men had not been making themselves up for our amusement but were on their way to some kind of gathering. Through our driver, who seemed nervous about the exchange, they asked if we could give them a ride. Not until we were underway did it occur to me that we might be dressed in war paint and on our way to war.

"You know, we could really get ourselves in trouble this time," I said to Darrell.

"You're right," he agreed, pointing his camera toward me. "Would you mind sitting a little closer to the guy with the nasty-looking tips on his arrows?"

Luckily, it turned out we were taking our new friends to negotiate a peace settlement, of sorts. Several hundred warriors from two opposing clans were gathering for a compensation ceremony in which our side had to pay thirty pigs for having killed one of the enemy warriors in an earlier battle.

Luckily, too, we arrived late at the big, open field where the ceremony took place, and many of the warriors had already drifted away.

Still, it made me think—seeing that some of the would-be combatants were not carrying bows and arrows but shotguns—that Papua New Guinea was not the kind of place you'd want to get into an argument over, say, your spot in line at a movie theatre.

And what if a battle had broken out? With everybody on the field understanding how payback worked, would a warrior go after an opposing warrior, knowing that doing so could bring down generations of retribution on his clan? Or would he go after the two pale-looking outsiders who, despite a little face paint, clearly had no clan ties at all?

* * *

Whatever the answer, I later wished that Darrell was along to help bolster my resolve on a visit for *Condé Nast Traveler*, to American Samoa, which had been hit by a killer tsunami so recently that everybody, including me, had a fresh story to tell about their experience.

My story began with the sun just rising, casting golden light on the slopes of the north end of Tutuila, American Samoa's main island, where I was alone, I thought, on the outside deck of Tisa's Barefoot Bar.

Sitting beneath palm trees along its own crescent-shaped cove, the bar was a rough-hewn structure that looked, with good reason, as if it was constructed almost entirely of flotsam and jetsam that had tumbled in over the reef guarding the curve of sand lying just below me.

Setting a self-brewed cup of coffee on one of the unpainted, weathered wooden tables and pulling up a chair, I found myself, as everyone else in that part of the Pacific had been doing over the previous few days, keeping one eye on the sea and one ear listening for ominous rumblings.

That morning, though, my senses were on alert even more than usual, the result of an evening's talk at the bar the night before that had ended with me receiving a gift from an American woman.

The woman, Kate Long, was an earthquake and tsunami specialist for the California Emergency Management Agency.

The gift was a refrigerator magnet that spelled out specific instructions about what to do if you were in a coastal area when an earthquake struck. Essentially, the instructions said not to wait for anybody official to instruct you but run for high ground as fast as you could.

Kate and her husband, Jeff Brandt, had come to American Samoa to study the after-effects of the tsunami. They were sleeping somewhere in the bar, where I also had a bed, because the handful of more conventional hotel rooms on Tutuila were occupied by scientists and disaster-relief workers who had arrived before we did.

My bed was in an open-to-the-sea, thatched-roof shelter that extended off the bar. And although the taxi driver who deposited me out front had offered to wait while I looked around, to make sure I really wanted to stay, I could not have been happier with the accommodation or the company. As Jeff said, Tisa's was a combination of *Gilligan's Island* and *Cheers*.

The previous evening, after the regular crowd had gone home, the three of us sat up late with the bar's owner, Tisa Faamuli, an American Samoan whose thighs were tattooed with what looked like a Southern Hemisphere star chart you could almost navigate by, and her husband, a ponytailed New Zealander who everyone called Candy Man. At some point, the conversation got around to discussing what most people actually do when confronted by the possibility of a tsunami, which, all four of my companions agreed, is to freeze, waiting to see how others will react.

Having had the benefit of that conversation, I was convinced that I would never freeze but instead hightail it for high ground at the first warning. This was an interesting bit of self-appraisal, considering what happened the next morning.

I was reaching for my coffee when the cup started to shake, first a little, sending dark waves racing around the coffee's surface, then violently, along with the entire table.

Desperately, I hoped that Kate, Jeff, Tisa, Candy Man, Darrell, anybody, would appear, preferably in some discombobulated state that would confirm I ought to be running. But no one showed, and I remained frozen, as if until the tide came in.

This is when I happened to look under the table, where a big, shaggy dog, in his great delight at having company so early in the morning, was wagging his tail so vigorously that he'd set the whole deck in motion.

* * *

The best near-death experiences, though, come when you least expect them, such as when I was doing a story for *Islands* magazine in the Philippines and was in the men's clothing section of a crowded department store on the island of Cebu. I was trying on a pair of jeans, which I needed because I had neglected to bring any from home for a journey that might require them.

The Philippines is a nation of some 7,100 islands. The two largest, Luzon, where Manila is located, in the north, and Mindanao, the Muslim stronghold, in the south, account for sixty-five percent of the landmass and sixty percent of the population. But I was planning to ignore these two and instead focus my visit on the Visayas, a centrally located myriad of palm-fringed, mountainous islands and islets connected by a network of passenger vessels that promised, as one guidebook put it, to "suit only those prepared to rough it."

To help in my preparations for roughing it, a smiling saleswoman had suggested I might be interested in a locally made brand of jeans labeled Canadian Club. I was trying them on in one of the store's curtained cubicles, and they fit fine, except for one small problem.

The hole that allows you to button your fly was sewn shut. I tried to explain this to the saleswoman, who followed me to the cubicle and was standing outside the curtain, repeating, "You like? You like? You buy? OK?"

But my explanation didn't seem to be getting through. So, perhaps sensing from my tone of voice that a sale was slipping away, the woman ripped open the curtain to see what the matter was.

"Oh, OK. No problem. I fix," she said, her smile becoming even broader. And with that, she whipped a razor knife out of a side pocket of her blouse, went down on her knees, and grabbed hold of the pants just above the missing fly hole. I, it is important to note, was still wearing the pants.

"No, no," I yelled and was immediately sorry. Among the people who came running toward the agitated foreigner who had a Filipina woman down on her knees in front of him with a razor knife in her hand was a store guard fumbling with a pump-action shotgun.

Luckily, the guard, perhaps sensitive to the criticism leveled against one of his colleagues a few days earlier for annihilating a shoplifter, did not shoot. In fact, once the situation had been explained, he was in the forefront of people rummaging through the stack of Canadian Club jeans looking for a pair in my size that didn't have the fly sewn shut. And he was mightily pleased when it was he who discovered one.

21

When Do You Know You've Been There?

Around the turn of the millennium, I was getting more assignments than I ever had, and travel seemed almost constant. On American Airlines alone, I reached million-mile status, giving me frequent-flyer perks that are supposed to last for the rest of my life, or American's, whichever comes first. And I circled the globe a half-dozen times, including once over a long weekend, for no other reason than to listen to the stories of fellow passengers.

For the weekend round the world, I stepped out of a taxi in front of JFK's Terminal 4 at five o'clock on a Friday evening to begin what my driver, at some risk to his tip, called the silliest journey he had ever heard of. And the woman behind the Air India check-in counter seemed to agree.

"Final destination?" she asked me, in a lilting Indian accent, without looking up from her computer screen.

"JFK," I answered.

She looked up. After just the slightest hesitation, she explained that she had not asked me for my departure point, which, she helpfully advised, was where we were now, but where my journey would end.

"JFK," I answered again.

She picked up a phone, put it back down, and asked, slowly enunciating each word, "How well are you understanding English?"

Soon enough, though, after scrutiny of my ticket and my passport by several levels of Air India supervisors, I was on my way. From New York, I touched down, briefly, in London, New Delhi, Bangkok, Hong Kong, Los Angeles, and Atlanta, and was back in New York on Monday morning.

A quirk of the journey was that once I departed New York, I did not leave an airport transit area, pass through a security checkpoint, or have my passport stamped by a government authority, until I was in Los Angeles. So, I never officially left the U.S., which initiated another interesting conversation at LAX's passport control.

During the forty-two hours I spent in the air, among the people I listened to were: A British woman returning from the funeral of a nephew murdered in Miami. A Mumbai computer programmer who argued convincingly for outsourcing U.S. jobs to India. Two women from L.A., one on the aisle, one by the window, who talked across me, for hours that seemed like minutes, about nipple rings. And an American businessman who professed to be baffled by the new rules of the workplace.

"Three separate suits against me for sexual harassment," he complained. "I just don't get it."

It was an entertaining trip, and it reinforced my belief in the usefulness of a recommendation I sometimes make to other travel writers. To double your chances of hearing a good story, always ask for the middle seat.

* * *

On other journeys, I visited Guam, Palau, and another island destination on the old Continental Micronesia Airlines route that I recall for the pleasure of sharing my briefest commentary on anywhere: "Yep, Yap."

On the same route, downwind from everything, I touched at Johnston Atoll, which, with people serenely bicycling here and there, looked like any quiet, small-town community. Except that dangling from each resident's belt was a gas mask. Abandoned now, Johnston was then home to the caretakers of the nastiest elements of the U.S. military's chemical and biological arsenal.

I explored Australia from the northern end of the Great Barrier Reef to Tasmania, and New Zealand from the Bay of Islands to Milford Sound, where I discovered, while preparing to cross a mountain pass on my hands and knees in winds blowing close to a hundred miles an hour, that the weather forecast along the Milford Track is always "promising."

I scuba-dived in the Cayman Islands, the Red Sea, and Vanuatu, in the latter learning that the *President Coolidge*, a World War II American troopship that succumbed to friendly fire, was not only the world's largest easily accessible maritime wreck but also the inspiration, during Bill Clinton's term as president, for a flourishing local trade in T-shirts emblazoned with the slogan "I went down on the President."

I defied death by crossing streets on foot at chaotic intersections in Ho Chi Minh City, cruised the Mekong River in long-tail boats, and tried to master, with a splashing lack of success, leg-rowing on Myanmar's Inle Lake. On the way to the lake, aboard a flight bumpy enough to cause a few people to scream, I thought how satisfying it would be to have my obituary record that I'd met my demise while flying Air Mandalay, on route to a town pronounced Hey Ho.

I sailed the Dalmatian Coast and the Turkish Coast. I marveled at Machu Picchu and the Taj Mahal. And I was shown the red cliffs of Jordan's Petra by Bedouins from the Howeitat tribe, who claimed to be direct descendants of people who served as extras in the making of the film *Lawrence of Arabia*.

I sea kayaked Fiji and Tonga. Hiked the Samaria Gorge and the footpaths of Cinque Terre. Mountain-biked the Trentino region of Italy and the arid countryside around Mexico's

San Miguel de Allende.

In the Egyptian desert, I first got to know travel writer Wendy Perrin, whose boyfriend, now husband, Tim, could have died when he fell down a dry well while we were climbing Mount Sinai in the dark. Sometimes, I can still hear the horrified screaming of the traumatized Bedouin who had been trying to sell us tea.

Again and again, I departed by ferryboat for one Greek island or another, always using as my guide the words of the Greek poet C.P. Cavafy:

As you set out for Ithaka
hope your road is a long one.

* * *

Some of those places, I visited for weeks, others, only minutes. Which I mention as a way to work in a story about Wallis and Futuna, an island territory of France so remote that I suspect even most people who live there wouldn't know where to find it on a map.

Flying from Tahiti to New Caledonia, we landed at the territory's main island, Wallis, just long enough for me to watch through the aircraft window as a little girl extended the welcome gift of a shell necklace to the wrong deplaning passenger, which increased the merriment of arrival for everyone but her.

Many travelers will say that because I did not get off the plane, I did not really visit Wallis and Futuna. Before you can check a place off your "Been There" list, they will say, you've got to be at a place a certain amount of time, usually, however long they themselves have been there.

Others will say you have to bring back some physical evidence: photographs, a stamp in your passport, branded items lifted from a hotel room, bruises from where somebody stoned you.

But by my measurement, as I think it should be for every travel writer, you have visited a place when you can return home with a story to tell.

* * *

I knew I had been to Belize, for *Islands* magazine, after spending an afternoon with seventy-three-year-old Lindsay Miller, who lived on a tiny Caribbean cay just off Belize's barrier reef.

"But, but...will it fly?" I'd asked Lindsay as I stood back to admire the eight-bladed contraption he had made from driftwood and other flotsam and jetsam he'd picked up on the reef surrounding his thatched-roof shack.

"She not supposed to fly," he cackled. "She supposed to shred de coconut."

Anywhere else, I might have taken the grizzled old man for just another aging fisherman, the years of his profession showing in his leathered face and the scars on his hands. But on his tiny island, I took him for nothing less than a mechanical genius.

The contraption, basically a windmill, not only appeared to be fully capable of doing what Lindsay claimed, but it was just one of several labor-saving devices he had created from what the Caribbean currents, and chance, had cast up to him. As I admired the sharpened fluke of an old anchor he used to remove the coconuts husks before the inner nut went into the shredder (and was eventually made into coconut oil he sold to passing fishermen), I asked where he got the ideas for his creations.

"De first ting, I get up in de morning and I have my coffee. Dat's number one," he said.

After a day of humid, mosquito-buzzing stillness, the wind had come up out of the north during the night, leaving Lindsay's sort of a windmill pointing in the wrong direction.

"If you ain't too busy, give me a help, and we can just swing her to de wind," he said.

He showed me where to put my shoulder against a beam on the creaking structure as he repositioned some wooden wedges. "All right, lady, come around, come around," he cajoled. And with surprising ease, the whole assembly pivoted. "Now we'll make her do some work," he said, loosening a rope here, pulling on a line there, until the whole wondrous contraption shivered to life.

"So, how often do you go into Belize City?" I asked as he fed oily white coconut meat into the whirring machine.

"Oh, every year, year and a half. But I don't care to. I had a lot of problems down dere because of too many people."

His solitary island, he said, was the life for him.

* * *

I knew I had been to the Isle of Man, in the Irish Sea, again for *Islands*, after I visited George Devereau & Son, Kipper Curers and Fish Merchants, just off the harbour-front in the port town of Peel.

"Is George Devereau in?" I asked after knocking on the door of a low, modern-looking building that seemed to be leaking blue-white smoke.

"In the ground," a young man in rubber boots and black bib overalls informed me. "It's Peter Canipa you'll be wanting to talk to."

My informant led me to a big, powerful-looking man, similarly dressed in boots and bib overalls, wheeling a six-foot-tall aluminum rack out of a stand-up smoker. Spiked onto the rack were neat rows of identically sized smoked herring, or kippers, all gutted and spread open and all a dark, golden brown.

"Have you had your kippers this morning?" Canipa asked me without preamble and was pleased to learn that my landlady had served them for breakfast.

"If you eat your kippers, you won't get half the things that go wrong with people," he said. "You won't have heart trouble. Bowel trouble. Kidney trouble. When I see people who don't feel well, I say to them, 'Here, get a kipper down you.'"

He stopped to light a cigarette. "People say smoking is bad for you. But I've been smoking forty-odd years, and I'm sixty this year, and there are not many fellas of twenty-one that will outrun me."

He handed me a steaming plate with half a kipper on it, keeping an identical half for himself. "I just wish you could try this with lime marmalade," he said. "Now that's the bee's knees."

* * *

I knew I had been to Eua, an outlying island of Tonga, for *Condé Nast Traveler*, when, on a Saturday night, a group of local men invited me to join them for an evening of kava drinking. With one of the men filling our shells from a communal kava bowl, and the three or four others casually cradling guitars, we sat cross-legged in a circle on the mat-covered floor of a community center.

There is some argument about the potency of kava, a drink made from the root of the piper methysticum plant and often described, accurately, as looking and tasting like dirty dishwater. Some say its effect is narcotic, others that despite the numbing of your tongue and lips, it does nothing more than relax you just enough so that you can discuss without rancor even the thorniest issues of politics, sports, religion, and women.

All I can say is that by, I don't know, two o'clock or three o'clock in the morning, we had all drunk ourselves into various stages of a stupor.

But here is the memorable thing. Throughout the night, any one of the men, his chin still on his chest, his body still slumped forward, would quietly begin to strum a note or two on his guitar. The notes would become chords, he would sit up, as if he were an electric appliance someone had turned on, and he would start to sing in the most melodious voice imaginable. That would bring the other men out of their slumps, and soon they would all be harmonizing to such effect that you wished you could take them all to Nashville and get them a recording contract.

A few hours later, everyone was in church, where I could tell from the tone that the sermon was fiery. But, not understanding the words, I was easily distracted by the ladies' hats.

* * *

And I knew I had visited Wallis and Futuna when I could tell the story of the little girl presenting her shell necklace to the wrong passenger.

22

Easter Island: a Mystery Solved, a World Found

Of all the places I've wanted to return from with a story to tell, Easter Island had been near the top of my list for so long that when I first started thinking about it, the islanders were probably still carving statues. I finally visited, for *Islands* magazine, with the usual curiosity about the enigmas and the usual skepticism about the theories to explain them.

I didn't believe that the statues, or moi, as the Easter Islanders call them, were created and transported by stranded alien astronauts who used them as rescue beacons. If that were true, such technologically superior beings would surely have been a little neater and not left so many broken pieces lying around. Nor did I necessarily agree with the locals, and most scientists, that the statue carvers had arrived from somewhere in Polynesia, far to the west, most probably the Marquesas.

My theory was that adventurer Thor Heyerdahl might have been right when he speculated that the carvers were the ancient Incas, who had created their own images in the work. Except that the Incas had been brought over, perhaps unwillingly, by the far more nautically adept Polynesians, who went and got them. This would explain why the face on every moi seems to be pouting.

Whatever theory might be correct, the story I brought back

from Easter Island was from an entirely unexpected source, as the good stories often are. And it helped me shed light on a mystery I'd been pondering since my earliest days of travel.

The story resulted from a conversation with a German woman who lived with a local artist in a hut overlooking the waves on Anekena Beach, where the Polynesians were supposed to have first landed on the island.

As we drank coffee out of tin cups at a table fashioned from gray driftwood, the woman insisted that the red stone topknots originally crowning many statues were not hats, as people often assumed.

"It is plain to see," she argued, "that a moi is an abstraction of a penis. So why would an erect penis wear a hat?"

It was a rhetorical question. Because before I could respond (And who cannot think of several scenarios involving an erect penis in which a hat might be useful?) she answered for me. "Because it is not a hat," she said. "It is a female sexual organ—on top."

As the woman spoke, I was reminded that islands give sanctuary to more than their share of odd ducks. In the animal kingdom, the Tasmanian devil, the Komodo dragon, and the late lamented dodo bird undoubtedly come almost universally to mind. But there are many other strange island-dwelling plants and animals. Scientists say all are the result of an isolation that allows them to develop without the homogenizing effect of universal influence.

In humans, the effects of isolation are not as pronounced because we are more mobile, having boats, bridges, planes, and, now, digital means of exchange not ordinarily available to devils, dragons, and dodos.

But being human, we also have the capacity for imagination. And the isolated, self-contained nature of islands makes it possible for people who are a little different, and sometimes more than a little, to imagine that here, finally, is a world they can begin to understand.

Alexander Selkirk was one of those people. And Robert Louis Stevenson. And a real-life figure that author Jack London describes in *The Cruise of the Snark*, his 1911 chronicle of a South Seas journey during which he is assailed, on Tahiti, by a beachcomber called The Nature Man, who has a two-fold message for saving the planet:

"First, let suffering humanity strip off its clothing and run wild in the mountains and valleys; and, second, let the very miserable world adopt phonetic spelling."

Another, whose story I would be able to make a part of my own, was Paul Gauguin.

* * *

In the 1880s, the French were employing thousands of workers for their ill-fated attempt to dig the Panama Canal, which was not completed until after the Americans took over in 1904. For about fifteen days, one of those workers was Gauguin, who in April 1887 arrived in Panama from France.

Ostensibly, the nearly penniless and unknown Frenchman had come to Panama in anticipation of working with his brother-in-law, who hoped to profit from the financial speculation resulting from the canal construction. But it is clear from a letter Gauguin wrote to his estranged wife, Mette, before he departed France, that his inclinations were otherwise.

"I am going to Panama where I will live like a native," he told her. "I know of an islet in the Pacific a league from Panama; it is almost uninhabited, free and fertile. I will take my paints and my brushes and rejuvenate myself far from the haunts of men."

The islet was Taboga, the first island I ever visited, on my first foreign journey, when I was sixteen.

It's unclear where Gauguin learned of Taboga, possibly

from Mette's family, who considered him an improvident nuisance they would have gladly directed toward any far corner of the earth. But it is clear he imagined the island, as he would later imagine Martinique and the islands of French Polynesia, as a world where he could become the person he was meant to be.

As with many of the experiences in Gauguin's life, Taboga didn't turn out as he imagined it would, largely because the island was far from "almost uninhabited."

Although barely two square miles in area, it had a pair of attributes—a protected harbor lying within easy reach of Panama City and a microclimate noticeably healthier than the mainland's—that had been attracting Europeans at least since 1524, when a catholic priest built a church there and founded a town, San Pedro.

The church, which still exists, and is said to be the second oldest in the Western Hemisphere, included among its early parishioners a couple whose daughter, Isabel Flores y de Olivia, conceived on the island but born in Lima, Peru, would become the New World's first saint. And the conquistadors who vanquished the Inca Empire sailed from Taboga's harbor. As did, perhaps, the pineapples that helped establish the Hawaiian pineapple industry.

A few decades before Gauguin's arrival, San Pedro had been made lively with boarding houses and even a theatre by fortune-seekers awaiting passage to the California goldfields. This is one of the reasons so many English names are said to be among the gravestones in the island's cemetery.

By the time Gauguin discovered Taboga, canal construction had so inflated prices on the island that the chances of an indigent drifter being able to buy a plot of land there, as he had hoped to do, were about nil.

"These idiots…will not let you have a yard of land for less than 6 francs a yard. It is impossible to build a hut and live on fruits without people mobbing you as a thief," he wrote to his wife.

The devil, he said, could take the people who had suggested Panama. And not long after, having produced no art that survived but still seriously enamored of islands, he sailed for Martinique, where he painted the first of the idyllic island landscapes that would make him famous, if not understood, or content.

* * *

On Easter Island, as I sat by the sea at Anakena Beach, willing at least to consider the argument that one of the planet's greatest mysteries might have to do with women on top, I recalled my visit to Taboga. I wondered if the lesson I had begun to learn there is that every traveler's life is a search for worlds we can finally start to understand.

* * *

But then, all our worlds were turned upside down.

23

Bali After the Bombing

On September 11, 2001, I was living in Manhattan with my third wife, Sally, who was the managing editor at *Brides* magazine, and our twenty-month-old daughter, Cleo.

I saw the smoke on that beautiful fall day and heard the first siren, then another, and another, until there was such a cacophony of them that I still cannot hear one without pausing to see if another will follow. Just as I cannot pass a fire station without looking for photos of fallen firefighters taped to a window or see a plane passing low overhead without pausing to reassure myself that it is continuing on its way.

For some time after that, every travel magazine wanted stories on destinations from which you could, if necessary, just about walk home. I wrote a few, set in Florida, Mexico, the American Southwest.

But for my taste, all those stories were too pedestrian. So, it was not until *Condé Nast Traveler* sent me to Bali following a terrorist nightclub bombing there in October 2002 that I once again felt I was a travel writer.

* * *

Here, according to the Balinese, is what happened on their equivalent of America's day of national tragedy:

There are good spirits in the world, and there are evil spirits. You can never defeat the evil spirits but only try to keep them in harmony with the good. In one common form, the harmony is represented by the black-and-white-checked cloths you see all over the island, even occasionally wrapped around the waist of an oversize stone statue of an Australian surfer.

On October 12, the harmony got out of balance on Bali, which the Balinese don't own, but only look after for the gods. And although the evil that prevailed came from outside, the fault lay with the Balinese themselves, who, perhaps because of their preoccupation with worldly success, or some other reason, lost their way and failed in their role as caretakers.

Afterward, through a series of cleansing rituals, they asked the gods to forgive them and bring their universe back into harmony.

* * *

And here is what I found when I arrived three months after the bombing, which had left 186 people dead, nearly half of them young Australian tourists targeted only because they were Westerners.

As I had discovered on other journeys there, the island remained one of the most beautiful, peaceful, and intoxicating places on earth. The mist still rose from the Ayung River. The terraced rice fields still turned emerald in the afternoon light. And the only safety concern I felt was from young men who seemed in a hurry to reach the next life by flying down rutted roads at night on motorbikes without lights.

Yet, Bali had become a sad place, too, because of the lives lost and because the Balinese had been made victims, in nearly the same way the September 11 tragedy had made victims of New Yorkers. The difference was that most New Yorkers did not depend on tourism for their livelihood, a livelihood that on Bali, for the moment, and perhaps even longer, had been all but taken away from the Balinese.

So why would anyone have wanted to visit Bali so soon

after the bombing? There were some selfish, perhaps not very admirable, reasons. You could have a beautiful, peaceful, intoxicating place almost free of other visitors. The tour buses were off the roads, and the restaurant guidebooks that said "Reservations essential" were out of date. You could get some incredible hotel deals. World-class five-star resorts were to be had for less than a hundred dollars.

But there was a far more important reason to go, too. You could learn something about how to live in a world turned upside down. Despite the hardship the Balinese had gone through and the uncertainty they might still have to face, I did not encounter a single one who was without the gentle graciousness or the disarming smile they have always had.

* * *

The first to smile was my driver, a fortyish, slightly round little man from the north of the island, where his older brother was still a rice farmer. His name was Made, a common Balinese moniker that means second-born. I hired him through a rental car company for ten dollars a day for a ten-hour day. If I wanted him to work beyond that, he said, I could pay him whatever extra I wished. It seemed like a good deal, although as he took what was obviously a wrong turn out of the airport, I did think to ask how long he'd been driving professionally.

It wasn't his regular job, he said. Following October 12, when almost everyone else at the rental car company had been let go, he'd had enough seniority to stay on. He did the paperwork on the three or four cars a week that might be rented. And when the rare opportunity presented itself, he hired out as a driver, a job for which he had no particular qualifications or, I realized by the time we reached my hotel, natural talent.

But he was such a gentle soul, and so obviously trying to make the best of a situation he didn't create, that even after he started to deliver me to the wrong hotel, I happily decided to keep him employed for all my time on Bali.

My first night, I stayed at The Ritz-Carlton, on an isolated stretch of coast just south of Jimbaran Bay, where guards used mirrors to check the car's underside for explosives. Welcome to the new world of travel, I thought. The next morning, as I checked out of the hotel, I realized I'd forgotten to arrange a time for Made to pick me up. But I found him waiting outside with the patience of someone who knew almost to a certainty that he had no other job prospects for the day.

He was the father of four children, the youngest a seven-year-old girl who, during normal times, insisted at every opportunity, but with only occasional success, that the family eat at McDonald's. The second oldest, a girl of nineteen, who he talked of often, always in the present tense, had died not long before in the hospital of causes he didn't fully understand.

* * *

We drove to Kuta that morning, to a little hotel across the street from the beach, within walking distance of where the bombing had occurred. The first time we drove by the hotel, its sign prominently displayed out front, I assumed Made was taking us to another entrance, or turning around, or something. The second time, I realized that I would have to point out the sign to him.

As I walked to my room through the hotel's inner courtyard, a young worker, his head wrapped in a black-and-white-checked cloth, was laying stones in the hot sun for a new pathway. It was part of a general refurbishing program, I would learn, that many hotels were doing just to keep people employed. Still, I thought, what a miserable job. He looked up at me and smiled.

* * *

Once a sleepy fishing village, Kuta had for decades been Bali's rowdiest resort, thanks largely to young Australians, for whom, before the bombing, it was the equivalent of a Mexican beach resort at Spring Break, except with more beer.

Stretched out along a sandy shore better suited for surfing than swimming, the town was a warren of shop-lined streets and alleyways. Lacking the masses of visitors that would normally support them, the shops offered distress-level prices on everything from woodcarvings to sex. But what you could buy most of were T-shirts. My favorite, almost as much for its faulty syntax as for its forthright message, was emblazoned with the words "F**k Terrorist," the strongest public rebuke of the perpetrators I would see or hear while I was on the island.

"How many of these shirts have you sold?" I asked a gap-toothed woman in one tiny shop just a few doors down from where the bomb had exploded. But the question seemed to go beyond her understanding of English because she answered that I could have three for eighty thousand rupiahs or about ten dollars.

"No, no thanks," I said, "I just want to know how popular these are."

"OK. Forty thousand."

Not to make too much of it, but the bomb site, which had come to be called Ground Zero by the locals, was as much a part of a visit to Bali as the World Trade Center site had become to a New York visit, with just as little to see. What had been the Sari Club, where most of the fatalities occurred, was a leveled lot, in front of which, on the day I visited, lay several bunches of wilted flowers.

"Why?" asked a tearful Australian standing next to me.

"Transport?" asked a Balinese.

The conventional wisdom for Americans traveling in potential trouble areas worldwide has become to maintain a low profile, avoid crowds, and keep your distance from any symbol of America. That night, though, feeling contrarian and curious, I visited Kuta's Hard Rock Café.

A very courteous uniformed guard frisked me, asked me to empty my pockets, and then ran a wand-type metal detector over my body. The precaution certainly diminished the likelihood that a terrorist could get inside. However, during the entire time I sat at the bar, if a bomb had gone off, the total number of customer fatalities could have been no more than one.

* * *

After I spent two days in Kuta, Made drove me north to the cool, green hills around Ubud. On the ride up, which we punctuated with stops at crafts villages where you could go straight to the source for stone statues, silver jewelry, and woodcarvings, two things in particular impressed me.

One was how serene the shopkeepers all seemed to be. Occasionally, a woman (always a woman) would invite me to look at her wind chimes, dragon kites, or theatrical masks with a gentle, "Come. Come. Only for looking." But mostly, they just smiled at my passing.

The other was the amount of vehicular traffic. The tour buses and rental cars were gone, to be sure. But you could still describe the roads as choked, especially with motorbikes. "I don't get it," I said to Made. "If there are no visitors, no work, and no money, where is everybody going?" He giggled in the way I had come to recognize as meaning he had no answer.

Ubud itself, while no sleepy hamlet, was where you went in Bali to find the heart of Balinese culture—dance, art, and the best of what is produced in the handicraft villages. It was where you wandered the streets, stopping in to examine an exquisitely woven wall-hanging or intricately carved sculpture, perhaps moving on to the Café Lotus or the Funky Monkey for a cold drink when you discovered that even in hard times, good art does not come cheap.

As I wandered, though, I noticed something curious, first in one shop, and then, when I started looking for it, many others. As I entered—where I would almost always be the only customer—lights, and perhaps a fan, would come on. And when I departed, they would go off. It was one more way, I finally realized, that the Balinese were attempting to get through the crisis, by conserving electricity when they could, but without inconveniencing visitors.

* * *

Departing Ubud, we spent a day searching for the perfect terraced rice field. Our exploration took us first to the base of sacred Mount Agung, whose profile is said to be the inspiration for the graceful arch at the top of the long, beautifully decorated bamboo poles that stand in front of practically every house on the island. From there, we went farther to the north and west, past the highlands lake district, where Made's brother, Wayan, or the firstborn, had his fields.

"What will you do if the tourists don't come back?" I asked Made that day, as he showed me his mother's house.

"Return here and grow some fruit trees for my family," he said.

I hoped he didn't have to, and I was sure he didn't want to. He'd made it clear, however, I might feel about it, that when he could, he liked taking his youngest daughter to McDonald's. So, a few days later, I was pleased when someone told me that the hundred dollars I would pay Made would allow his family to live for a month or more.

And a few days following that, after he dropped me off at

the airport with a smile as warm as the one with which he had greeted me, I was pleased again, as he pulled away, to see that he was headed in what appeared to be the right direction.

I only hoped that the same was true for his beautiful, peaceful, intoxicating Bali.

24
My Limp?
Dogsled Accident.
In Greenland

Joan Tapper was gone from *Islands* magazine. Barbara Fairchild was out at *Bon Appétit*. And no doubt influenced by the Internet's effect on our attention span, demand for long narrative pieces of the kind I had specialized in was fading.

Yep, Yap.

I did still occasionally write longish articles for *Condé Nast Traveler*. They were assigned by Dinda Elliott, a veteran editor but new to the magazine, who wanted more that had to do, appropriately enough, with how the world was changing and how people were adapting to it.

One of my stories for Dinda began in Ilulissat, a town on the west coast of Greenland, about 150 miles north of the Arctic Circle. I arrived in late March, near the end of winter, when the days were growing long again but the sea ice was still solid enough, I had been assured, to support the weight of a dog sled.

On just such a sled, my guide, Johannes Mathaeussen, and I were about to set out on an adventure across a white, treeless landscape. The sled, little more than a narrow wooden platform on runners, was piled about three stories high with gear and supplies. Included among it was a shotgun whose barrel I kept catching a boot on when, for practice, I climbed atop the pile, where I was to ride, Johannes told me, "like a cowboy."

Our twenty-dog team, appearing to know that they were about to hear the word to do what they were bred for, which was to run, were yapping excitedly and straining against the metal ice screw to which their traces were still attached. But Johannes—whose Danish-sounding name resulted from Greenland's long-time status as a dependency of Denmark, and whose flattened Inuit features were from a bloodline that originated, untold generations ago, somewhere on the high, cold steppes of Mongolia—was for the moment ignoring them.

Staring thoughtfully at the sky in the direction of the coastal hills we would soon be ascending on our way to the frozen fjord on the other side, he finally said to me, "Snow is maybe coming."

"How do you know?" I asked, following his gaze but seeing no clouds or other signs I assumed his lifetime of surviving in that desolate land had taught him to read.

"Internet."

His answer gave me pause, but I knew it shouldn't. For thousands of years, Greenlanders—almost all of whom can claim to be some mix of Inuit—had been forced by nature to live such a tenuous existence that they still often appended statements of intent or desire with the word immaqa (maybe). And in all those years, the one thing that had allowed them to survive was their ability to adapt.

"If the snow comes, what do we do?" I asked, having researched our adventure well enough to have vivid images of myself in an Eskimo Pie-like state of permanence.

Flashing me a grin that revealed a missing tooth or two, forty-six-year-old Johannes—who for most of his life had been a professional hunter and ice fisherman but who, like many of his contemporaries, had in recent years supplemented his income by taking tourists on dog sled adventures on the ice—pulled up the hood of his parka and pretended to be shivering.

The parka highlighted, I couldn't help but observe, the contrast in our sartorial styles on that fifteen-degrees-Fahrenheit morning.

I was standing there in the clothing the local company that had brought us together insisted I rent from them: sealskin pants and parka that were certainly warm enough, balmy, in fact, especially under the arms, but made me look and smell like a stuffed animal.

On the other hand, Johannes was wearing layers of moisture-wicking, water-repelling, color-coordinated gear from the likes of Patagonia and The North Face, gear that wouldn't have made him look out of place if he were trying to survive in, say, a Starbucks.

However well Greenlanders, all 56,000 of them, had mastered the art of adaptation, though, their skill was being tested more than ever. Because there, on the world's largest island, just over eighty percent of it covered by an ice sheet up to 1.6 miles thick, climate change wasn't a theory but an observable fact.

* * *

For most travelers, witnessing climate change in Greenland meant a summer visit aboard a cruise ship to Sermeq Kujalleq, the Greenlandic name for the Jakobshavn Glacier, a UNESCO World Heritage Site whose prodigious and increasing output of melting ice from the great inland ice sheet had made it a symbol of global warming. (Not to mention that it may have produced the iceberg that sank the *Titanic*.)

There was another change to be witnessed, though, and—at least until the international oil and mining companies who were arriving on the scene discovered what the receding ice sheet might have to reveal—it would have more effect than any other on traditional Greenlandic culture. That change was the disappearing sea ice.

"Ten years ago, we had sea ice for nine months of the year, and now less than half the year," a Greenlander named Ole Jorgen Hammeken told me a few days earlier, as I admired the collection of Inuit artifacts on the walls of his home in the western Greenland village of Uummannaq. (Who knew there were so many types of seal-skinning knives?)

Scientific observation corroborated what the Greenlanders had seen for themselves. During the summer of 2008, satellite imaging recorded that the area of the Arctic Sea covered by ice shrank to the second smallest it had been since satellite monitoring began in 1979. There was less summer ice only in 2007, when the Northwest Passage, in the Canadian Arctic, was ice-free for the first time in human memory. That year, the ice shrinkage broke the previous record by twenty-five percent.

And there was something else Greenlanders had seen for themselves. North of the Arctic Circle, which included three-quarters of Greenland, the disappearance of the sea ice for longer and longer periods was threatening wildlife—notably the polar bear and the narwhal—important to traditional Greenlandic communities. It was also causing the decline of another critical element of Inuit culture, sled dogs (which are used primarily on the ice), since many Greenlanders no longer bothered to keep them. The last was particularly unsettling, Ole Jorgen said, because in Greenland, "a man doesn't feel like a man if he doesn't have dogs."

Thousands of dogs remained, though, and there was no more dramatic way for visitors to witness climate change and experience traditional Greenland than by dog sled. That's assuming you didn't mind the smell of dog, on everything, and were willing to camp on the ice in a sleeping bag rated, one really should insist, to minus forty degrees.

* * *

Which is how I came to be there, on the outskirts of Ilulissat, it's scattering of boxy houses painted green, yellow, red, or blue against the bright white of the ice, as Johannes turned from his contemplation of the sky and focused his attention on the dogs.

Earlier that morning, I'd chatted about sled dogs with Aleqa Hammond, Greenland's finance and foreign affairs minister. I'd met her in line for the breakfast buffet at Ilulissat's almost-five-star Hotel Arctic, where I hoped she didn't notice that my survival skills included stuffing my pockets with hard rolls in anticipation of the trail ahead.

I'd told her that one of the things I hoped to accomplish on my journey was learning to drive a dog team. At which Aleqa, a straight-talking woman, rolled her eyes and asked, "How far can you run, in the snow, wearing boots?"

Secretly, I'd been offended. But now, watching Johannes' team of twenty dogs, which, it had been pointed out to me, was a handful even by Greenlandic standards, I decided that another of Aleqa's attributes might be her wisdom.

Unlike their Alaskan and Canadian counterparts, Greenland dogs are not usually harnessed in tandem, two by two, but in a fan pattern of traces. And in the few moments of Johannes' distraction, his dogs, as incapable as a group of kindergarteners of lining up in an orderly manner, had made a rat's nest of their traces. But with the aid of a few kicks so enthusiastically applied that in some jurisdictions, they might have resulted in jail time, he soon had everything sorted out to his liking.

"Sit down, please," he said to me, and, before I could get both of my heavy gloves under the lashings I was supposed to hold on to, we were off, one of my arms uncontrollably waving in the air like a rodeo rider's.

* * *

In a few minutes—the dogs finally all at work, the sled's runners making a swooshing sound as they cut tracks through the snow—Ilulissat disappeared behind a white fold in the landscape. And a few minutes beyond that, I was made to realize, with great force, that a dog sled journey—which, around there anyway, required a trip over white-clad hills before you could get to the sea ice—was not something to be taken lightly.

After a gut-wrenching struggle to the top of a pass, I arrived feeling like I'd breathed my last breath about a hundred yards back, trail etiquette having required me to help out the dogs by jumping off the sled and loping alongside in my planet-Jupiter-weight boots. My satisfaction at seeing Johannes also gasping for air turned to apprehension, though, when, after re-positioning the dogs so that they were behind the sled—as though they would be needed to act as a brake—he motioned for me to climb back on.

Looking over the crest at the icy trail falling steeply away from us, one side bordered by a cliff face and the other by a sheer drop, I hesitated. "OK?" I asked doubtfully, as in, "Are you sure this is safe?"

"Cowboy," he answered with emphasis, as in, "Come on, be a man."

So, I climbed atop the gear, and down we went, not losing control until almost at the bottom, when one of the sled's runners caught the edge of a lump of ice, I threw my weight in the wrong direction, and we flipped over spectacularly. The sled came down hard on my right foot, causing me to howl so loudly that even the dogs seemed impressed.

After righting the sled and untangling the dogs, Johannes shuffled back to where I was lying face down in the snow. "OK?" he asked, as in, "Am I going to have to give back my guide fee?"

I got up, took a few tentative steps, and decided—after

briefly considering the consequences of having my story end there—that I would be able to go on.

"Ok," I answered, as in, "I'll survive," despite a leg I would limp on for the next six weeks.

He again gave me his gap-toothed grin and happily shouted what I would come to recognize as a favorite English expression among the handful he knew: "Extreme Greenland!"

After a few more ups and downs, all of which I managed to get through without being pitched into the snow, we were out onto the flat sea ice of the fjord. In a couple of months, it would be open water. But for now, I beheld a frozen kingdom ringed by steep white hills and domed by a blue sky (the snow predicted by the Internet having gone elsewhere) that appeared to be ours alone. I decided one nearly crushed foot was a small price to pay for the privilege of entering such a place.

* * *

Our plan—contingent, as everything was in Greenland, on the weather and the condition of the ice—was to circumnavigate the fjord before heading south toward Sermeq Kujalleq, the glacier. We wouldn't be traveling east to the inland ice sheet itself because, except for a few scientists and death-wishing cross-country skiers, hardly anyone went there, not even the Inuit, as it was essentially a lifeless, featureless, frozen desert. Still, even though we were on the twenty percent of the island that at least occasionally uncovers itself in the summer, it too was then pure white wilderness—without towns, without villages, without trees, and, we hoped, without signs of melting.

We drove north along the fjord for several hours, the only hint that anyone had ever been there before us a faint track of trampled snow our dogs followed with only an occasional word or crack of the whip from Johannes. I knew it was cold out because the batteries in my digital camera quickly died.

But bundled in my seal skins and protected by my gloves, ski goggles, and boots, I had less complaint about the temperature than I had a few weeks earlier, at a Mexican beach resort, where the evenings were a bit cool for my liking.

As we rode, me mostly lost in a state of dream-like contemplation, I found it hard to imagine that any change could ever happen there or that the rest of the world could care.

Around noon, I was awakened from my reverie when we stopped on the ice for lunch: coffee from a thermos and sliced bread spread with potted meat that I suspected had traveled farther than I had to get there. The meal was memorable, though, and the reason was the view.

Locked in the ice before us was a single towering iceberg, white, pink, and blue. It looked so much like a medieval castle, complete with turrets, spires, and archways, all sculpted by the warming sun, that I almost expected to see flags flying from it.

"OK?" asked Johannes, as in, "Wasn't this worth the effort of getting here?"

"Beautiful," I answered, giving him two thumbs up to help with the translation.

* * *

Late in the afternoon, we drove the dogs off the ice and jogged alongside them up a snowy slope to a cabin where we would spend the night. It was not much of a cabin—more like a metal shipping container with a door cut into it. But while Johannes fed the dogs from one of the sacks of dried food that we were lugging along with us, I got the Primus stove going and soon enough was once again reminded that I'd felt colder in Mexico.

Dinner was musk ox, an animal that looks something like a wooly mammoth but is related to the goat—perhaps due to some youthful indiscretion during the last Ice Age, when its wanderings took it as far south into North America as what is now Ohio.

Taking a bowling-ball-size chunk of ice, Johannes dropped it into a big pot and placed it on the stove. When the ice had melted, he added the musk ox, which he'd hacked from a frozen slab with a cleaver and diced into two-inch squares. Next came a few handfuls of rice and half a large plastic bag of vegetables, which, it goes without saying, were frozen.

"Musk ox for ten," I exclaimed when he handed me a steaming bowl.

We ate with such relish that I had to revise my estimate downward to "Musk ox for four," the two leftover portions going to the dogs. As it also turned out, though, the dinners that would follow—including reindeer and halibut—would all be prepared in exactly the same way.

The meal over, we rolled out our sleeping bags on a plywood platform, first cushioning it with foam pads and reindeer skins. And even though there seemed to be a reindeer hoof somewhere up around my nose, I was soon asleep. During the night, I woke only once, at the sound of some disturbance among the dogs. And I was awake only long enough to remember that polar bears were usually found farther north and, with the thinning sea ice, becoming harder to find anywhere.

* * *

The morning was another ride across flat ice. Johannes sat on the front of the sled, puffing away on his pipe for mile after mile, the smoke and ash blowing back at me as if from the stack of a coal-burning locomotive. I didn't mind, though, protected as I was by my ski goggles and my seal skin parka pulled down over my forehead, because I had learned to recognize that when the pipe was going, all was right with the world. It was only when Johannes hastily knocked the ashes from its bowl, stuffed it in a pocket, and sat up straighter, that I knew I needed to pay attention.

He put the pipe away once when the dogs, apparently sensing something about the ice they didn't like, were hesitant to continue. "Bad," he said to me—not of the dogs but the ice—and, relying on their judgment, we headed in a new direction.

He put it away, too, when we were riding alongside a jumble of ice at the edge of a cliff. Spotting a movement that brought his hunting instincts to the fore, he dragged the sled to a halt and pulled his shotgun from beneath the straps. Sighting on something I couldn't see, he fired, and a snow-white bird tumbled out of the rocks high above and came to rest at the foot of the cliff.

Johannes motioned for me to go get it, but I hesitated, eyeing the uneven ice between the bird and me.

"Cowboy," he urged.

With misgivings, I headed toward the cliff, Johannes' thumbs-up signal growing ever smaller and less reassuring. But I retrieved the bird without incident, and Johannes stuffed it under one of the straps at the front of the sled.

A few minutes later, he saw another bird, and we went through the same process, except this time he handed me his whip and went after the bird himself.

I was watching him, idly wondering how long I would survive if he fell into a crevasse, when out of the corner of an eye, I saw a flash of brown. I turned just as a dog lunged for the first bird. With a snap of its powerful jaws, he swallowed all of it but one severed, dangling leg, which was still strapped under the lashings.

I took a step forward and raised the whip, causing the beast to turn toward me with bird in his bared teeth and murder in his eyes.

"Just kidding,' I said, "Just kidding," as I lowered the whip and slowly backed away.

The dog was still watching me when Johannes returned with the second bird. When I explained what had happened, he laughed, removed the one remaining leg from the lashings, took a bite of the raw meat, and handed the bloody remainder to me.

I hesitated just long enough to consider how much of a wimp he already thought I was, then took a tentative nibble.

"Extreme Greenland!" he exclaimed.

That night, we pitched a tent that Johannes dubbed Hotel UNESCO, a name I suspect he had used with success before. Set atop a slight rise, it had a commanding view of a miles-long madness of convoluted ice—giant blocks and shards twisted in every imaginable shape. We were looking at Sermeq Kujalleq, the Jakobshavn Glacier.

* * *

The next morning, we rode almost to the edge of the glacier, where, to my surprise, there was a camp (seemingly abandoned) of four tents identical to ours. Near each tent was a hole about three feet long, eighteen inches wide, and a foot deep. In front of each hole was a hand-cranked metal drum on a frame, with a heavy green line leading from it down into the sea, which had a skim of new ice. Near one of the holes was what looked like a towel rack, on which gutted halibut were drying.

"Fishermen," said Johannes, pointing vaguely in the direction of Ilulissat, at nothing I could see.

From the rack, he took enough halibut for a meal for us and in its place left a plastic grocery bag containing what I could only assume was of equal value in the emptiness of Greenland: a pouch of tobacco and a roll of toilet paper. I expected that we would then be on our way. But instead, Johannes took out a nail file and clippers and began giving the dogs a pedicure.

The dogs were lolling around on the ice as if they were

expecting a massage next when the fishermen returned, four of them, each with a sled. They were soon winding in their lines, which, they told me, mostly using figures drawn in the snow, were a quarter-mile long, with maybe 150 baited hooks on them.

The men offered me the opportunity to crank in a line myself, and, just before my knees buckled from the effort, one of them took over again, and fish started coming up through the ice—the first of fifty or sixty twenty-pound halibut.

"Extreme Greenland!" exclaimed Johannes as the soon-frozen fish piled up beside the holes.

I lay back on the ice, looking up at the sky, listening to the voice, from a fisherman's CD player, of Nat King Cole singing "Little Girl," and thinking that I could not imagine a more idyllic experience. But it was made even more so, at least for a moment, when a flock of those snow-white birds flew over.

Then, blam, blam, blam. Three shotguns fired, and three birds were on the ice. To each his own idyll, I guess.

* * *

We spent the night in a cabin similar to the first day's, except it was bigger, and we shared it with a pair of Danish women and their two guides, all of us wedged up against one another on a wooden sleeping platform, in the Inuit fashion, or so the guides claimed.

Although it was a long evening of conversation, mostly in Danish, my only recollection of note was that there is nothing like sleeping in close quarters with women of slight acquaintance, and who would have been quite attractive in any circumstance, to make you realize how desperately you need a bath.

* * *

In the morning, Johannes and I headed back over the mountains toward Ilulissat. During the ride, we saw no one until, just before we got to a snowy field behind the Ilulissat power station, where his dogs and hundreds of others were kept, we passed a young Inuit couple walking hand in hand along the trail we'd just traveled.

I felt I'd gotten a glimpse of a traditional way of life that might literally be melting away. I was even pleased with my limp, since, in the following weeks, it would allow me to bring almost any conversation around to how I injured myself in a dog sledding accident, in Greenland.

As was probably true of every visitor who had seen and been touched by that unique place, I was concerned for it. After all, new signs of climate change were constantly occurring. I had no idea how all this would affect the way Greenland looked in a hundred years or twenty or the next decade. Or what it would mean for the rest of us. Yet, when I gave Johannes a tip that I felt he well deserved, he was so profuse in his thanks, swearing he would spend it all on dog food, I suspected that no matter what changes global warming might bring, Greenlanders would continue to adapt just fine.

25

Camp Jaguar.
All Welcome.
Except for Snakes

The Greenland story seemed to please *Condé Nast Traveler* enough that they asked me to do another about global change from a local perspective. This time they wanted it focused on a rainforest. Ideally, I suspected, again involving an experience that might put my life at some risk.

So, here I was, shortly after sunrise on a humid January morning, standing alongside the Burro-Burro, a cocoa-colored river that meandered through the heart of a nearly pristine rainforest in the South American country of Guyana.

I had just stepped ashore from a battered, outboard-powered, canoe whose three other occupants, all native rainforest dwellers, had nudged onto the river's steep, muddy bank. All three had declined to step ashore with me, but one did have some last-minute advice. "As long as you have a fire, it's OK," he said. "You'll have no bother from the mosquitoes, the spiders, the snakes, and"—he paused, with what I hoped was not uncertainty—"the jaguars."

The speaker, Lionel James, whose name and fluency in English were the result of now-independent Guyana's British colonial past, was a member of a tiny group of indigenous people known as the Makushi. For the past week, I had been in the rainforest with a half dozen Makushi hunters as they tried to teach me how to survive without the conveniences—and even, some might argue, the necessities—of modern life.

Then, to see if I had been paying attention, they were abandoning me on my own for a few days along a section of the river far from our already remote camp. I was without food or shelter and had with me little more than a machete, a flint for starting a fire, and a small bottle of iodine to kill (most of) the undesirables in the river water I'd be drinking. For life-threatening emergencies, I also had a two-way radio. But what timely assistance I would be able to summon if, for example, a jaguar had me clamped by the neck was unclear.

As I ascended the bank, my machete drawn and my steps tentative, an overhead limb almost immediately snagged the Indiana Jones-style hat that I thought looked so fitting when I'd first tried it on at a post-Christmas sale at a mall in the States. I suppose I should have considered it my first victory that the branch wasn't a snake.

"See you soon, maybe," said Lionel as they pushed the boat back into the river.

"Maybe," reluctantly agreed the boat's driver, Sparrow, who, I couldn't help but observe, had the cover off the outboard motor, as if there was some problem that might signal its approaching demise.

The insects were buzzing, and the ripped piece of an old T-shirt I wore as a sweatband was already soaked. But except for those minor discomforts, which I had come to ignore, it was a beautiful country the Makushi had set me down in. The scent of orchids perfumed the air. The leafy canopy was alive with flashes of color from birds and butterflies—red-and-green macaws, blue morphos, tiny, almost iridescent, hummingbirds. Somewhere not far off, howler monkeys were holding a lively discussion, probably about me.

The question was why anyone would willingly let himself be left alone out there and—what most puzzled my new friends, the Makushi—even pay for the opportunity.

* * *

Guyana, not to be confused with its neighbors, Suriname, which is the former Dutch Guiana, and French Guiana, of Devil's Island fame, is one of the smallest and poorest countries in South America. If outsiders know anything about it, they most often have only a vague recollection of an infamous (and no-longer-existent) community called Jonestown. In 1978, more than 900 members of a religious cult, many of them Americans, committed mass suicide at Jonestown by swallowing a lethal potion. The act has the dubious distinction of often being credited as the source of the expression, "Don't drink the Kool-Aid."

But Guyana did have another distinction: Ninety percent of the population, including the people living in the capital, Georgetown, were crowded onto a narrow, Atlantic-facing coastal strip already so prone to flooding that it would undoubtedly be among the first places to fall victim to a rising sea level caused by climate change. However, most of the rest of the country, where only the Makushi and a handful of other native groups lived, was covered by one of the few rainforests in the world considered to be nearly intact. (Papua New Guinea and the Congo were home to the other most notable.) And Guyana's then-president, Bharrat Jagdeo, was determined to keep it that way, even if it meant turning over almost all his country's rainforest to the supervision of an international body.

I was there, I had convinced myself, because if I were to understand the solution Jagdeo suggested well enough to write about it, I first had to experience the rainforest in the most unfiltered way possible.

How unfiltered that might be was a point, I admit, I was having trouble keeping focused on just then, because as I pulled at the branch that had snagged my hat, something dropped softly onto the back of my neck and I was instantly, painfully, bitten. When I slapped my assailant to the ground, I saw that it was a hairy brown spider only an inch or so around but with legs so thick that if it had been a professional athlete, I would have immediately suspected it of using steroids.

Perhaps disappointingly to *Condé Nast Traveler,* the spider bite was not fatal, causing only a lopsided swelling of my neck and a welt that would last for several weeks. But, to continue....

* * *

For the world to keep breathing, rainforests, which are in effect the earth's lungs, must survive. They absorb carbon dioxide and either store it, thus helping to moderate the greenhouse effect, or convert it, through photosynthesis, into air we can breathe.

In most parts of the world, however, rainforests were being gobbled up by development—logging, mining, farming, and, in the Amazon especially, cattle ranching—at such a rate that their loss contributed as much to the annual increase in atmospheric carbon dioxide as the worldwide emissions from cars, trucks, and buses combined.

Guyana's rainforest, though, had remained almost untouched, the reason being the difficulty of getting at it. Innumerable waterfall-punctuated and rapids-strewn rivers tumbling off the interior highlands had presented a so-far insurmountable challenge to building any but a few roads and bridges. The main north-south artery through the rainforest, the "National Road," was unpaved red clay, cut in one place by a river that could only be traversed by a rusting car ferry. The road was so unforgiving to vehicles that when I traveled it by bus from Georgetown to a rendezvous where the Makushi waited for me, a fellow passenger said as I boarded, "You'll want a seat that's still bolted to the floor."

But as technologies advanced and economic pressures mounted, developers were beginning to cast covetous eyes. Plans were in the works to turn the National Road into a genuine transportation link through the heart of the rainforest, allowing industries in northern Brazil access to the port in Georgetown. Such a connection would bring unprecedented change.

* * *

In the natural way of things, change was already happening. I could see that in the tiny village of Surama, in a savannah-like clearing at the edge of the forest, where my Makushi companions lived. Although still mostly thatched-roof, dirt-floored huts without running water or electricity, the village of about 225 people had a community center from whose sometimes-functioning TV the villagers learned that a black man, Barack Obama, had been elected president of the United States. And they thought they learned (the BBC coverage having been confusing on this point) that a woman, Hillary Clinton, had been elected vice president.

Hunters from the village had been offering guided forays into the forest for several years. And there was a community-owned lodge where travelers who didn't mind having only intermittent electricity and were untroubled by the occasional bat flying in through the unscreened windows could be quite comfortable.

As a result, it had been some time since the Makushi painted their faces in preparation for a hunt or stalked the forest in nothing but loincloths. Instead, one Makushi—Hendrix, who was Lionel's brother—favored a black T-shirt emblazoned with the image of a guitar and the words "The Jimi Hendrix Experience." Another, Harold, the oldest and most versed in forest lore, carried, possibly with no intentional sense of whimsy, a Barbie backpack.

That growing awareness of the outside world was a good thing, said Ian Craddock, a forty-two-year-old former British special-forces army officer who owned Bushmasters Amazon, a Guyana-based adventure company that took a handful of clients into the rainforest each year to learn from the Makushi. It meant that culturally the Makushi were at the only stage that made possible the kind of exchange we were having.

"If they were any less developed, it would probably be better to leave them alone, and if they were any more developed, they would probably no longer have their forest skills," Ian said as we joined the Makushi for a few beers—as a preventative against mosquito bites, they told us—on the eve of our departure into the rainforest.

* * *

With us as we departed Surama the next morning—a harpy eagle circling overhead and mist covering the tops of the surrounding hills—were three other Bushmasters clients, all men in their thirties and all looking for adventure.

At least there were three of them to begin with.

On the first day, while setting up the base camp where we would live for a week with such luxuries as hammocks and cooking pots, we lost Steve, a Londoner, who early money had pegged as the toughest of the Bushmasters. He decided he'd had enough when the Makushi, for a little joke, wrapped a deadly—but dead—snake around the rope from which he'd suspended his hammock.

"I've learned all I need to know," he said and headed, we suspected, for Barbados.

I wasn't sure that Phil, another Brit, would last long either. He just seemed so unsure of himself, at first jumping at the rustle from every leaf pile. Which, in the rainforest, will keep you very jumpy, indeed. It did say something for his determination, though, that he made it through the week despite neglecting, just once, the Makushi's admonition to shake out his boots before putting them on and as a result crushing a tarantula with a socked foot.

Vlado, a Slovakian native but living in New York, was, on the other hand, irritatingly competent. While the Makushi struggled to show Phil and me how to build a fire, Vlado would already be sitting in front of a three-foot-high blaze, roasting piranha on a stick as if they were marshmallows.

Piranha was a staple of our diet, supplemented by military-style MREs (meals-ready-to-eat) that Ian had supplied. Catching the fish, using machetes to crack open rotting nuts to get at the white, undulating grubs we used for bait—and knew we had to eat if the fishing didn't go well—was one of the survival skills the Makushi taught us.

"You really eat these?" I asked Lionel after he'd convinced me, for the experience of it, to bite into a grub.

"When we have to," he said.

"And when did you last have to?"

"Oh, ten, fifteen years ago."

* * *

By the end of a week, we had familiarized ourselves with how to build a shelter, how to start a fire with flint, how to hunt with a bow and arrows we'd made ourselves, how to trap various—and I so wish this weren't so—large rodents, and how to minimize the greatest danger: severing one of our own limbs with our own machete.

In the evenings, early enough so that we wouldn't get caught out in the dark, we'd cool off by bathing in the river.

"Why don't you worry about the piranha?" I asked Hendrix one evening, recalling a story in which a school of the toothy fish had skinned a wading horse alive. "Or the caiman?"—a member of the alligator family that reportedly grows up to twenty feet long. "Or the anaconda?"—a snake that can be large enough to make wrestling with caimans seem like the preferred alternative.

"Because it's better to worry about the electric eel," he answered.

* * *

What the Makushi thought of our efforts is hard to say, although chuckling often accompanied exchanges in their language when one of us did something like let go with an arrow that traveled no farther than the toe of our boot.

Nor was it clear, even though they professed to be opposed to such destructive activities as indiscriminate logging, if the Makushi truly believed the forest could be in danger of disappearing.

"It goes without stop to Georgetown," one of them told me. Georgetown, where most of them had never been, being their measure of a place almost inconceivably remote.

* * *

And I had to admit, as the puttering of the outboard—taking Vlado and Phil to their own lonely outposts—faded until the sound of flapping wings masked it, I could see their point. In perpetual twilight because of the thick canopy overhead, a seemingly endless rainforest of extraordinary biodiversity was all around me, with plant and animal species numbering in the thousands.

Among my neighbors were plants that had played a role in developing anesthesia. There was a bird, the hoatzin, so primitive that it was born with claws at the end of its wings. And somewhere out there was the jaguar—the biggest cat in the Western Hemisphere—which wasn't necessarily using a figure of speech when it thought, "I'm so hungry I could eat a horse."

Remembering the warning to keep my bow always with me and my arrows always ready, because you never know when a large rodent might amble by, I took a few tentative steps into the gloom.

To survive in the Guyana rainforest, you need to know, I had been assured, only half a dozen plants. One, which I spotted right away, was the water vine, a tree-climbing woody shrub that looked like kinked rope. After a few whacks with my machete, it produced a brief fountain of water sweeter than any iodine-laced river brew.

Just beyond the water vine, I spied a manicole palm, which had a pulpy heart that tasted like cabbage would if you were really hungry. That particular tree also had, about six feet up the trunk, the distinctive striations the Makushi had taught us to recognize as scratch marks made by the claws of a jaguar—one, I hoped, that was giving itself a pedicure and not marking its territory.

My most valuable discovery, though, was a Kokerit-palm. Not only did the nuts that fell to the ground host the grubs that were such an inspiration for finding other sources of food but its big leaves were just right for the roof of the shelter I would build: a sleeping platform high enough off the ground so that snakes and peccaries (a wild pig whose razor-sharp tusk and nasty disposition made it more feared than jaguars by the Makushi) could pass under without being put in a confrontational mood.

As I selected four young trees—spaced the right distance apart to form the corner posts of my shelter—and started trimming them with my machete, I remembered a warning from

Hendrix not to get carried away with home building. "Simple. Simple," he'd repeated, clearly understanding, as President Jagdeo also apparently did, that development is not easy to stop once it gets started.

I, unfortunately, did get carried away. I made my sleeping platform king-size, built a tower annex up which I could climb at the first foul whiff of approaching peccary, carved a sign reading, "Camp Jaguar. All Welcome. Except Snakes," and dragged a felled tree down to the river, where I planned to cut it into sections I could use as the foundation for a boat dock with which to greet the returning Makushi.

By the time I finished, I was exhausted and soaked in sweat. I poured a few hatfuls of river water over my head to cool down and lay on my sleeping platform for just a brief rest. I told myself I'd begin gathering wood and getting a fire started in a minute.

Except that my short rest turned into an afternoon nap. When I awoke, the light was already fading, not because it was dusk, but because it was about to rain—a torrential rain that lasted until it really was dusk, leaving me with having collected hardly enough firewood to roast a hot dog, if I'd had one.

Not that it mattered. Despite all the tutoring on how to scrape dry kindling from an inner layer of dead but still-standing hardwood trees, and despite having set up my fire area under the shelter itself, the rain had so saturated everything that I couldn't have started a fire right then even if I'd had a blow torch.

Then very quickly, it was dark. Can't-see-your-finger-on-the-end-of-your-nose-dark. Wish-my-survival-skills-had-included-smuggling-in-a-flashlight-dark. And I was back on my sleeping platform, because even the Makushi said they didn't like to be afoot on the forest floor at night.

At first, every time I heard something moving through the undergrowth, I reached for my machete, which I'd hung within arm's length from the nub of a lopped-off branch on one of the shelter posts. A couple of times, when the rustling got close, I pulled the machete out of its sheath and banged it against the post, wishing I knew whether such an unnatural ringing was more likely to serve as a deterrent or a dinner bell.

Soon, though, I recalled the risk of the machete to me. So, I lay back, my hat pulled over my face to discourage mosquitoes, and tried to think pleasant thoughts, such as that Phil and Vlado might also have failed to get their fires started.

I was about to nod off when I was jolted fully awake and grabbed for my machete again. Loud enough to make me wish I too were in Barbados, I heard the distinctive sound, almost like a loud cough, that a jaguar makes. Having been told that they like to go for the back of the neck, I used one hand to hold my hat tightly to it, hoping the smell of the hat's sweat-soaked brim would be as offensive to the jaguar as it had been to Phil and Vlado. But when I heard the sound again, it was fainter, as if the big beast (they can weigh up to 350 pounds, this one being all of that, I was sure) was on the other side of the river and moving away from me.

I drifted in and out of sleep until finally, accompanied by a rising chorus of howler monkeys, frogs, and unknown insects, the black of night rapidly turned to the dark grey of dawn. When I could see beyond the shelter posts, I was struck again by how beautiful my surroundings were—now all soft, fresh-washed shades of green, each leaf tip ending in a crystalline liquid globe. But with thunder promising more rain, I saw little chance of getting a fire started. I thought about that, thought about it some more, then dug out my radio and called Ian to ask that he send the Makushi for me.

It was not, I told myself, that I particularly feared spending any more nights in the forest without a fire. It was just that I'd had that experience, and, like Steve, I'd learned all I needed to know, which was that one night was enough.

Camp Jaguar. All Welcome. Except for Snakes

* * *

When the boat arrived, preceded by the sound of its outboard motor, I was surprised to find that along with Lionel and Sparrow, Vlado, our most competent Bushmaster, was aboard.

"I came back last night. There was no problem, but I was lonely," he said.

He didn't volunteer anything more, and I didn't ask, for fear it would bring the conversation around to inquiries about how I'd gotten on with my fire-making.

We waited a day, a night, and part of another day before the Makushi went after Phil, telling him we really needed to be getting back.

When we were united again, Phil, all bright and cheery, said that being alone in the rainforest, sitting around his fire, nibbling on a piece of piranha he'd smoked, was such an incredible experience he was going to ask Ian if he could stay on and work for him.

"Great idea," I said. Then I turned to Vlado and asked if he wanted to trade for the spaghetti and meatballs in his meals-ready-to-eat pack.

Later, Ian told me that you never know who will stick it out alone in the rainforest and who won't. Just like you never know, when the planet is in trouble, and the rainforests and oceans and atmosphere must be saved, who will step up and take the lead.

26
The Places Farther Out

I went back to the Maldives, where so many years previously the possibilities of a travel writing life had opened for me. And where people were now keeping an eye on the tide, in the most low-lying country in the world, for fear that one of these times it might come in and never go out again.

I returned to Tahiti, where I had been so often that on the ferry to Moorea, I had a chance conversation with a local who casually asked why he hadn't seen me in a while.

And *Condé Nast Traveler* sent me deep into the Sahara Desert, where the small band of Bedouin I traveled with on camelback for days across the dunes were amused that I wore my cheche, a turban-like head covering, so ineptly that I was at constant risk of setting an unraveling end of it aflame in our campfire.

But then, much more than my head covering began to unravel.

* * *

In 2012, *Brides* magazine, which *Condé Nast* published, let go most of its senior staff, including my wife Sally, and replaced them, it seemed to me, with people whose primary qualification was a claim of proficiency with social media. Shortly afterward, *Condé Nast Traveler* made a similar move, eliminating virtually everyone on the staff who had ever listened to my voice, and possibly silencing it on those pages forever.

Over time, and for much the same reason, most of my other once-dependable travel writing outlets dried up, too. As they did for a majority of my contemporaries, far too many of whom thought that they might be able to regain relevance by creating a website or writing a memoir.

* * *

Sally, who has had to make her own adjustments to the digital and pandemic upheavals, is now a new-media maven based in Scottsdale, just outside of Phoenix, where we have family and live on the edge of the desert in a community that can best be explained by noting that the mascot of the local elementary school is the scorpion.

Considering my nearly life-long preference for what Herman Melville calls "the watery part of the world," Scottsdale is not a place you would think I could easily call home. And it is true that sometimes about the only way I can make it through the day is to take out a jar of Long Island Sound water whose collection was my last act as a resident of New York and contemplate the depth of the green sludge that has settled at the bottom.

I admit, though, that I like the mornings of desert hiking and the evenings of desert stargazing. And I like the elemental feel of the desert, which is not unlike the elemental feel of the ocean: the breadth of the sky, the intensity of the sun, the movement of the wind, and, on occasion, the sparkle and flash of the tattered remains of abandoned mylar birthday balloons.

Sometimes, I even write about my desert surroundings, as I did in a piece for *The Ritz-Carlton Magazine* that begins like this:

* * *

Covering much of southern Arizona is a desert made distinctive by towering cacti that grow naturally nowhere else. The desert is the Sonoran, and the cacti are the saguaro, who often raise their arms like those of Old West stagecoach passengers accosted by outlaws.

I hike in the Sonoran Desert almost every day, whether in Scottsdale's McDowell Sonoran Preserve, which at more than 30,000 acres is the largest urban preserve in America, or further afield, such as in Saguaro National Park, whose trails, near Tucson, include one, Signal Hill, leading to petroglyphs that look like thousand-year-old graffiti.

Contrary to the impression many people have of the desert as dun-colored emptiness, unchanging beneath a relentless sun, I have discovered on my hikes a landscape as varied and as beautiful as any on the planet.

* * *

I like to think the message of that story is you can make a world for yourself anywhere, no matter how different it might be from any other you have known. And as my ode to the desert might suggest, we are not living a bad life in Arizona, especially now that I have enclosed our backyard with a snake fence.

But once in a while, usually after I've yet again been reminiscing about Zanzibar or Antarctica or Papua New Guinea for our Scottsdale neighbors, among them golfers, desert gardeners, and advocates of open-carry handguns, someone will ask if there is anywhere I haven't been that I'd like to return from with a story to tell.

Almost always, I immediately think of Más Afuera, the speck of land deep in the Pacific Ocean, a hundred miles west of Robinson Crusoe Island, and wish I'd been irresponsible enough to jump on the Chilean supply ship that offered me passage there.

I might think, too, of Pitcairn Island, St. Helena, and Tristan da Cunha, all for their mid-ocean remoteness. And Timbuktu and Kathmandu, just for the sound of their names. And the South Pole, because who has landed on the shores of Antarctica without wanting to go the extra miles?

Looking up into the desert sky, I might also include the moon. And Mars. And maybe most of all, one of the worlds near the edge of the Milky Way, where everything is likely to be a little different, and maybe more than a little.

And I will answer, "Yes, all the places farther out."

ABOUT THE AUTHOR

Bob Payne is an award-winning travel writer who has visited more than 140 countries. His travel humor has appeared in publications that include *Outside, Men's Journal, Islands, Bon Appétit,* and *Condé Nast Traveler,* where he was a long-time Contributing Editor and is believed to be their only writer ever to put the cost of a Polynesian tattoo on an expense report. His work has been called notable by the series, *The Best American Travel Writing.* A passionate admirer of oceans and islands, he lives in the desert in Scottsdale, Arizona, where on occasion the only way he can make it through the day is to take out the Mason jar of Long Island Sound water whose collection was his last act as a resident of New York, and contemplate the depth of the green sludge that has settled at the bottom.

CONTACT: bob@bobcarrieson.com

Praise for
ESCAPE CLAUSES

Bob Payne has literally gone to the ends of the earth during the long career as a travel journalist he so entertainingly chronicles in *Escape Clauses*. Thanks to the people he meets along the way, his adventures are funny, amazing, sometimes scary, always memorable. The stories he tells take you on the journey of a lifetime.

JOAN TAPPER
former editor of *Islands* Magazine

Travel writer has long been one of the world's most enviable professions, and Bob Payne's *Escape Clauses* demonstrates why. He brings to this charming, far-flung memoir all the humor and surprise of travel itself.

THOMAS SWICK
author of the *Joys of Travel: And Stories That Illuminate Them*

Escape Clauses is a rich account of a life well-traveled. Bob Payne, however, is no ordinary traveler, and his storytelling is dense with detail about trips that often go sideways. He strikes up conversations with people the rest of us might ignore or even sensibly run away from. In so doing, he gets his story, from pursuing the ghost of Alexander Selkirk on Robinson Crusoe's island to taking a leisurely swim at the North Pole. And if there are pickpockets, slow moving ferries, or clear-cut dangers, so much the better.

EVERETT POTTER
contributor to *National Geographic Traveler*
and creator of *Everett Potters Travel Report*

Made in United States
Orlando, FL
10 March 2024